ICAS:

15O YEARS AND STILL COUNTING

A CELEBRATION

Published by
The Institute of Chartered Accountants of Scotland
CA House, 21 Haymarket Yards
Edinburgh EH12 5BH

First Published 2004
The Institute of Chartered Accountants of Scotland

© 2004
ISBN 1 904574 09 2

Printed and bound in Great Britain by
TJ International Ltd.

CONTENTS

Appendices

PREFACE

The idea behind this book was a simple one. It should celebrate not just the 150th anniversary of ICAS but also the character of the institution and its members.

So it is not a history in the textbook sense. It does contain ten chapters looking at significant issues, at turning points in the ICAS story and at the development of the profession in recent years. But scattered through the intervening pages are a mass of other items, some extraordinary, all exceptional. Some follow themes. Others simply reflect particular events or people and their times. The aim was to provide a book which could be read straight through but which could also be enjoyed, as one past President of ICAS would put it, as 'a dipper'.

Editing such a book and writing large chunks of it has been an immensely pleasurable task and I have been guided by one principle. While researching in the ICAS Library I came across an account of the Glasgow Institute dinner in March 1933. My grandfather, Sir Robert Bruce, then in his last years as Editor of the *Glasgow Herald*, gave the speech on behalf of the guests. There is no detail of what he said. But *The Accountants' Magazine* described it as 'one of the happiest speeches of the evening'. I hope that the same happiness spreads to the readers of this book.

Robert Bruce
Editor
October 2004

Acknowledgements

The Scottish Chartered Accountants Trust for Education provided funding for this publication to celebrate 150 years of The Institute of Chartered Accountants of Scotland.

With grateful thanks to Ian Marrian, Aileen Beattie, Nigel Macdonald, Ron Paterson, Stephen Walker, Richard Anderson, Isobel Webber, Dorothy Hogg, Bridget Bell and many others for all their help, guidance, encouragement and assistance.

INTRODUCTION

CONTINUING TO INSPIRE

BY

IAN ROBERTSON
ICAS PRESIDENT

I hope the reader will find that this 150th anniversary publication provides an appropriate and readable insight into the history and character of The Institute of Chartered Accountants of Scotland. The variety and format of the recollections and reflections affords the opportunity to go "behind the scenes" in terms of how ICAS has developed over the years – but also why it has been able to develop in the way it has.

While, of necessity, such a publication as this derives much value from looking backwards, ICAS is of course very much alive and well and looking to the future. Indeed our most recent strategy review was entitled "Fast Forward to 2010". I have therefore been reflecting on where all the history you read here has brought ICAS as it reaches the grand old age of 150. What is the present day ICAS and what does it stand for? What are we proud of – other than our longevity?

One of the things that any President of ICAS soon discovers is the high regard in which ICAS is held around the accounting world and the business community. ICAS not only has a long and distinguished history, it has a reputation for high standards in education and research, and for thought leadership in accounting. It has a reputation in the international accounting world for punching way above its weight.

We are proud of the efforts we have made in recent times in emerging nations in Africa, and with fledgling economies in Eastern Europe, to set up the basis for future growth in such places by providing accounting infrastructures and showing them how to develop accounting professional bodies such as ours. We have worked in thirteen countries over the last ten years.

We are proud of the major effort we have put into research work and of the reputation that work has justifiably earned ICAS in terms of thought leadership in the accounting world. We have delivered 53 publications over the past sixteen years. This work has provided the initiative and underpinning for much of the governance and financial reporting structures which have emerged in the UK, and which continue to influence strongly, world-wide developments in these fields.

We are proud that the agenda for the development of accounting standards in the UK over the last 15 years was set by an ICAS publication – *"Making Corporate Reports Valuable"* – published in 1988 and authored in part by one David Tweedie who went on to chair the UK Accounting Standards Board that delivered on that agenda.

We are proud that a lot of the thinking on modern day auditing practices was outlined first in another ICAS research paper *"Auditing into the Twenty-first Century"* published by ICAS in 1993.

We are proud of the successes of our members and their influence around the accounting world. David Tweedie (now Sir David) now chairs the International Accounting Standards Board. Paul Boyle – another of the team which wrote *"Making Corporate Reports Valuable"* – is now Chief Executive of the Financial Reporting Council in the UK. Past Presidents Macdonald and Percy are key originators of the modern day corporate governance regime in this country and another Past President Sir Robert Smith recently chaired the committee which produced the Smith Report on the work of Audit Committees – a major contribution to UK corporate governance.

Not bad for a wee Institute from Scotland – to paraphrase one of our eminent Past Presidents!

The challenge now is, of course – follow that! – and what ICAS has been doing over recent years is planning how to do just that.

Internally we have reorganised our management, committee and governance structures to ensure we are fit for purpose and following best practice.

We have examined in great detail the issues we see ourselves, the profession, and the business world facing over the coming years and set out a strategy to address them.

We have identified Education, Regulation, Continuing Professional Development, and Member Engagement as key planks of that strategy and are working – and indeed starting to deliver – on numerous ways of taking these forward.

We have recognised Thought Leadership as the key differentiation of ICAS and are working on the identification of the key issues and ideas for the future – and how to fund and resource research into them. One example of this is our 150th Anniversary Conference entitled "*Seeking the Truth in Tomorrow's Business Environment*" – which seeks not only to tackle the thorny issues of the role of accounting in the global economy which now exists, but also seeks to provide an agenda for our future research and the development of accountancy's involvement and engagement internationally.

The scale of that topic is indicative of the breadth and depth of thinking which ICAS involves itself in and the taking on of the challenge of such a topic is indicative of the deep desire at ICAS to be at the forefront of the development of accounting in years to come.

But from all this plethora of ideas and issues I would like to end by looking at what I believe to be the two most fundamental to ICAS – our membership and our reputation. And I suspect in that I am merely echoing what has been said in many different forms by my many predecessors over the years.

One issue which, for ICAS, is unique to the early part of the 21st century is the impact and effect of the growth of ICAS membership. If our present pattern of training continues then within eight years our membership OUTWITH Scotland will outweigh that within its bounds. I see that – not as a threat - but as a wonderful opportunity. But it is one which has to be nurtured in many ways.

One of the keys to success will be to ensure that all our members – both within and outside Scotland - feel part of ICAS, and we are well aware that that will require great commitment. The Institute is as relevant and forward thinking as it has ever been and its members – whose active participation has always been one of ICAS's main strengths - are contributing in ever greater numbers to the issues of the day - working to further ICAS's reputation and always with regard to the public interest. I hope we can continue to inspire them so to do and to continue in the footsteps of those distinguished members I talked of earlier.

Another way in which we have to nurture our increased spread of activities is to look at the business case for increasing ICAS involvement in professional and commercial activities in other ways. This is a process which we are constantly working on. Speaking personally I believe that while we must always balance the risk against the rewards, we must be brave enough to move on into new areas of activity, if only on the grounds that the alternative is stagnation and growing irrelevance. Those are things we do not intend to let happen.

Finally, I have talked in detail about ICAS – past, present and future. At the end of the day however the members of ICAS do not join the Institute to serve themselves, or even ICAS. We exist to serve the public interest. That interest can only be served if we – and the whole accounting profession - can maintain its reputation in the eyes of the public we seek to serve. The reputation of the whole profession has been damaged in recent years by events internationally and - regrettably – here at home too.

Much work is being done to restore that reputation – from International Accounting and Auditing Standards, research on ethical issues, and making compulsory, continuing training for our members. Without the trust of the public we cannot fully serve them.

I would therefore exhort every individual member to do nothing in their day to day work which would in any way damage their reputation or that of the profession.

Let us all work together to ensure that the ICAS motto – "*Quaere Verum*" – "Seek the Truth" - truly reflects the public perception not only of our activities but of the profession as whole.

Only if we constantly work together in this way can we say with certainty that ICAS will be held in the same high regard in 2054 as it most certainly – and justifiably – is today.

Ian Robertson
President
October 2004

Early Days 1: Under the Hat

The Scottish Institute of Accountants' (an early competitor of ICAS's predecessor bodies) publication *The Scottish Accountant* produced an insight into the days of the founding of what is now ICAS when in July 1897 it fell to reminiscing:

> *To illustrate the advance made by the profession during the last fifty years, it may not be out of place to mention the state of matters as they existed in Greenock near the beginning of that period. There were then no accountants in that town, but certain individuals who had been clerks in mercantile offices and had a knowledge of accounts were temporarily employed in lawyers' and merchants' offices to do accountant business, when the ordinary staff of the office could not overtake it.*
>
> *I well recollect one of these peripatetic accountants, who was occasionally employed in the office in which I served an apprenticeship to the legal profession, and who from the facial resemblance to the first Napoleon was better known by the soubriquet of "Napoleon" than by his own name. He was a clever man, but had certain failings which on occasions prevented him timeously carrying through the work he had undertaken. On one occasion when he was thus engaged he became very restless and made the pretext that important business required him to go out. Although strongly remonstrated with, as the work he was at was wanted at once, he made off crying as a parting salute in his most grandiloquent style that if the governor wanted him, he would find him at the "Broken-hearted" Club, a rendezvous so called because it was the resort of men who "drowned their sorrows in the flowing bowl". He was a strange mortal this "Napoleon", and would sometimes say he would get through his work more quickly if he was allowed to take it to his office. The*

clerks who knew he had no office sometimes teased him by asking where it was when he would take off his hat with a great flourish, scattering its contents, which was a snuffy pocket handkerchief and a bundle of dunning letters mostly unopened, and would exclaim with great emphasis, "My hat is my office!". To emphasise quite how great a change had occurred in the intervening fifty years the author then points out that: *'Modes of conducting business which might be tolerated fifty years ago would not do in this year of the Diamond Jubilee of Queen Victoria, nor is it necessary it should for even in the smaller provincial towns, members of the Scottish Institute and of other societies may be found able and willing to undertake professional work, and have it finished punctually and efficiently, to the utmost satisfaction of those who employ them'.*

So there.

Newfangled 1: Blotters Win

Sir John Mann CA, gave a detailed picture of advances in business in the days of his CA father in the 1850s in a Centenary article he wrote in 1954.

The equipment was primitive, as exemplified in the handling of correspondence. Goose quills, requiring frequent "mending" with pen-knives, squeakingly preceded steel nibs; both envelopes and matches were scarce and dear, so outgoing letters were folded and closed with wafers: on high occasions they were closed with wax and sealed with fob and signet rings. Blotting paper slowly vanquished sand and the pounce box. Dictation was very rare — no shorthand. Important letters were often drafted in pencil in longhand and given out to be extended in beautiful copper-plate. Exact copies were also made before despatch in large bound folio Letter Books which were duly indexed. Even in those leisurely days there was sometimes a rush for the post, and any rough copies were laid aside to be recopied later into the Letter Book. Then someone found that sugar added to the ink made it sticky enough to yield exact copies of the original when carefully covered with loose sheets of damped paper squeezed in a copying press. It took care and adroitness to secure readable press copies, to be copied by hand into the folio books; but they so accumulated that finally the press copies were bound into books and replaced the manuscript books. Although my father was one of the pioneers of shorthand writing and taught it to me – it was, he said: "Sometime like a third hand" – yet he did not use it in the office. I sometimes used it and have found that a clever typist can read my notes, when often I cannot read them myself.

Four Generations of Haldane CAs

by

Martin Haldane

I suppose that I was born into the accountancy profession, as my father, grandfather and great grandfather were all chartered accountants. It was perhaps inevitable that I should follow in their footsteps. My great grandfather, James Haldane, indeed became a member of the Edinburgh Society in 1856, less than two years after its formation, and thus my roots go back almost the full 150 years which are presently being celebrated. James Haldane was assumed a partner by Donald Lindsay and George Auldjo Jamieson in 1858 in the firm which became Lindsay Jamieson and Haldane and remained as such until the mid-1960s, when on amalgamating with Richard Brown it became Haldane Brown & Co before joining Arthur Young McClelland Moores & Co in 1970. My grandfather, Herbert William Haldane became a partner in 1898, my father, James Haldane in the early 1930s and I became a partner in Haldane Brown & Co in 1968. When Haldane Brown were moving in Edinburgh in 1969 from St Andrew Square to Abercromby Place I found a post office directory which the fly leaf showed had belonged to Donald Lindsay, and on which he had written his address. It turned out that the firm was (until then unknowingly) moving back to the building where Donald Lindsay had first put up his plate in 1823.

As well as being born into the accountancy profession I was also fortunate enough to be born into a branch of the Gleneagles Haldane family and we, indeed, were known within the family as "those who went to add up in Edinburgh". The firm of Lindsay Jamieson and Haldane very much had its roots in the landed interest as Donald Lindsay was a landowner in Angus. When I joined the firm in Edinburgh in 1968 there was still a room in 24 St Andrew Square called the Factory Room, although factoring of estates had long since given way to work in relation to their tax and accounting. There were few of the large agricultural estates in Scotland whose business in some way did not occupy those working in 24 St Andrew Square, and agricultural estates were still a major part of the business of the firm when I joined.

From the mid-nineteenth century onwards the firm was prominent also in the financial services field: Clients over the next century included The Bank of Scotland, The Royal Bank of Scotland, Scottish Widows Fund, Scottish Provident Institution, North British and Mercantile Insurance Company and Scottish American Investment Company, the earliest investment trust to be based in Edinburgh. In addition George Auldjo Jamieson and my great grandfather were Liquidators of The City of Glasgow Bank which spectacularly failed in 1878. Industrial and commercial audits included the forerunners of United Biscuits and Scottish and Newcastle Breweries and, in London, Johnson Matthey and Bowthorpe.

Although born into accountancy, my coming of age was certainly not painless. Coming down from Oxford with a respectable degree in Politics, Philosophy and Economics and an inflated idea of my own capabilities, being asked as a junior apprentice to deliver the banking round the town and to take charge of the postage book was certainly a culture shock. Promotion in due course to the mundane audit tasks of 'bumping and ticking' and comparing final accounts to the original drafts did nothing to boost my morale, and I nearly gave up my inherited profession at least a dozen times in the first six months. But then I was only paid £300 in my first year, rising to £350 in my second and £400 in my third year, and I suspect all apprentices staved off the terrible boredom with extramural activities in the 'back room' and an excess of time charging to 'General Business'. Writing this at the time of the Golf Open Championship I recall however a pleasurable assignment. A band of apprentices, including myself was dispatched to Muirfield, home of the Honourable Company of Edinburgh Golfers, one July to assist in checking the cards of competitors in the Open. Not only were the arithmetical skills required relatively undemanding (even without the yet to be available hand held electronic calculator), but an opportunity was afforded to us to mingle with the great of the golfing world. I recall Jack Nicklaus sitting in the Recorder's caravan reliving every single shot of his round before he would entrust his score card to me for the seal of audit approval.

Although the social side, if one may so describe it, of apprenticeship was fun, the training really was an awful experience – and this is no criticism of the firm where I was indentured; it was the same everywhere. Thank goodness that has changed with technology and improved audit techniques. Much else has changed, mainly but not entirely for the better. Interestingly in the nineteenth century the independence of the auditor was by no means the concern it is today, or, as I prefer to see it, it was taken so much for granted that it was not necessary to prohibit the auditor from acting in different capacities. In the late nineteenth century my great grandfather as auditor of Scottish Widows would step in and act for the general manager when he was away. In 1883 my great grandfather was appointed auditor of the North British and Mercantile while his partner, Mr Jamieson, was a director. My great grandfather was a director of the Royal Bank of Scotland while one of his partners was the auditor. This of course is now against the law, but practice is far ahead of the law and I believe that partners responsible for public interest audits are now required or are about to be required to rotate every five years. What has happened to the rewarding (to both the client and the accountant), relationship built up by a skilful honest and dedicated professional whose knowledge of the clients business adds value by balanced advice without the professional in any way losing his independence? That kind of relationship cannot now, as a result of the actions of a few unprofessional chartered accountants, be created by the auditor, who should be in the best position to provide knowledgeable support. The shadow of Caesar's Wife extends a long way.

I can imagine my forbears opining that this is the result of the profession having relinquished the characteristics which that name implies. I well remember being told, on informing an enquirer that I was going into the accountancy profession that I would have an interesting but not too stressful life but would not of course expect to earn the money commanded by those who went into industry. Tell that to a senior partner of a Big Four accountancy firm. I also remember the horror in the mid–1960s, when an Edinburgh accountancy firm arranged to have its name in heavy type in the Telephone Directory. Advertising was of course then strictly prohibited as inappropriate to a profession. The idea of national, far less multinational, partnerships would have been inconceivable to the pioneers of the accountancy profession, for whom a close knit group of like minded individuals who knew each other well would have seemed the ideal unit for providing professional services, and there are still of course firms who operate on that basis; they are not however those which for obvious reasons carry most weight in the profession – or should we call it business?

The early days were not without their excitements. My grandfather's charmingly old fashioned notes about the first hundred years or so of Lindsay Jamieson & Haldane include a description of "the dastardly treatment of Mr More by Somervell of Sorn". Francis More was a partner in Lindsay Jamieson and Haldane and was acting as Somervell's Trustee in Bankruptcy in 1902, when Somervell arrived at 24 St Andrew Square when the office was relatively deserted over the lunch period and fired a shot at him in his room, luckily however doing him no lasting damage, although Somervell was convicted of something less than attempted murder and sent to prison for a while.

Now having retired from practice, (although not from dealings with accountants), it is interesting to look back over more than sixty years of involvement in some way with the profession, from going into 24 St Andrew Square as a boy where so many people seemed almost part of an extended family, through a problematic training system to partnership in an international and then subsequently in a more local firm, where many of the potential perceived conflicts of interest were mercifully absent. The main impression I am left with I think is how reactive in one sense the profession is, and I suppose this is entirely to be expected for a service profession; it reflects the changes in its clients. On the way, again inevitably, it has parted from its roots, its ethos of, to some extent, disinterested service and become as business-like as its clients, competing like them and using the same techniques to secure advantage, while at the same time trying desperately to retain the distinctive badge of a profession and the public esteem that goes with that term.

For the record Martin Haldane served his apprenticeship in Chiene & Tait. George Chiene, founder of that firm, had served his apprenticeship with Lindsay Jamieson and Haldane. He became a partner in Haldane Brown & Co in 1968, having been on the staff in London for two years. As a result of amalgamation he was a partner in Arthur Young McLelland Moores, latterly Arthur Young, until 1989 when he joined Chiene & Tait again, this time as a partner. His circular career provides an interesting perspective on the changes in the accountancy profession over that period.

Scots Outwith 1: The Parsee

For many reasons Scots chartered accountants have famously been successful all over the globe. And they have, for well over a century, sent back reports of work in exotic or dangerous lands, from the days of the Empire right up to present wartime work in Baghdad. George Cecil reported on 'The Parsee Accountant' in March 1901. 'In Bombay', he reported, the Parsee Accountant 'reigns supreme'. 'Indeed', reported Cecil, 'he will be found ready to undertake the unravelling of the deepest mysteries in connection with neglected and badly-kept books'. The working hours were from ten until half-past five and 'when not engaged in the manipulation of figures he woos slumber. For the Parsee is a believer in domestic economy and pleasure may, in the land of nod, be obtained at an ideal price'. 'Cricket and football are also indulged in by him, and at the former pastime he is as successful of an evening as he is during the working day with his pen and ready-reckoner'. Cecil was impressed all round. 'One may briefly sum up the character of the Parsee accountant by observing that he is quick at figures, intelligent, neat, and clean, to the seventh place of decimals, scrupulously tidy in his habits, invariably honest, and exceedingly polite'. And unlike his fellow contemporary Scottish accountants: 'He is strictly temperate and a non-smoker'.

Early Days 2: Scandals

Research by Stephen Walker in 1996 revealed a scandal which showed how early accountants were not necessarily the strait-laced and painstakingly honest folk of Victorian legend. One Donald Smith Peddie started to practice as an accountant in 1831 and joined the newly formed Institute of Accountants in Edinburgh in 1853 becoming a member of Council from 1872 to 1876. During the 1870s he backed various business ventures run by one William Cornelius. It all ended in tears and a series of legal actions in which they both claimed debts and unpaid fees from each other. Cornelius then issued a summons against his wife and Peddie in an action for divorce. This claimed that Peddie, then in his mid-sixties and a council member of the Institute, had been having sexual intercourse with Cornelius's wife Elizabeth in his office, at the Cornelius residence and 'various other locations'. Cornelius sent the following letter to Peddie:

> *My long felt suspicions are then now at last realised into Truth, the enclosed is a Copy of one of your corruptious letters written by you to my wife, I might have sent you a Copy of an other one, but they are all so filthy, so much so that I do not like to soil my hands with them. These are the deeds committed by D S Peddie, Esq., my particular friend, who has gone every Sunday to Church, I say read this letter you fearful monster, you come as a Wolf in Lamb's Clothing to my house, why could you not leave me alone. Satan look at your destruction, what have you made of my poor Wife: a hur, a hur corrupted with your filthiness, poor soul. God have mercy on her and forgive her. Do now what you like, you have done your utmost. If the Law of this Country would permit me I should know how to deal with you, give me satisfaction and do not turn a coward in the bargain. I am entitled to revenge and will have it. I shall have some of this letter printed in large type and post them up on walls, yes even on the pulpit of your Church.*

A court case was to follow. But before it could Cornelius received a letter from Peddie in London saying that 'he was obliged to go home for a few days'. He was then rumoured to be in Spain. His property was sequestrated and he was bankrupted, as was Cornelius. In his absence, and after further examples of his frauds had come to light, a warrant for his arrest was issued in December 1882. A lurid wanted poster was issued by Edinbugh City Police offering a reward of £100. He was described as 'an accountant, 74 years of age' and possessing a 'Scotch accent' as well as 'a furtive look and a reserved manner'. In January 1883 *The Times* newspaper reported that Peddie 'was buried in Philadelphia two months ago in Potter's Field, under the name of John North'. Some good did come of the affair. In that same month the Council of the Institute resolved to create a byelaw which would give Council 'power to expel from the Society, any member who is found guilty of Breach of Trust, fraud or misdemeanour of a similar kind'. The rule came into force in February 1884.

Early Days 3: The Character

David Murray, in his *Chapters in the History of Bookkeeping, Accountancy and Commercial Arithmetic*, published in 1930, records an early example of Scots feeling that their duty was to bring proper accountancy to the English. He describes how one David Browne headed south to London in the mid-seventeenth century and set up as a teacher of accounts above the Unicorn in St John's Street. He took the view that Scotland was rather superior to all other nations when it came to learning and he summed up the reasons for this as:

1.   *Scotland was never conquered.*
2.   *It hath the greatest succession of Kings.*
3.   *Scottishmen are the most excellent warriors.*
4.   *Scotland is the best fortifier of other nations.*
5.   *The Roman Emperors wall of defence from the Scotts.*
6.   *Scottishmen are most completely bred and farthest travelled.*
7.   *Scotland is an exact abridgement of the whole World.*
8.   *Scotland can best serve itself without traffick.*

9. *Scotland hath the strongest buildings.*

10. *And the rarest monuments both natural and artificial of any country.*

11. *And to crowne all the rest, Scotland made the most religious covenant of any nation since the dayes of the gospel in the happy reigne of King James of blessed memory.*

He offered to teach people to keep accounts in only one month.

Scots Outwith 2: The Hindu

In August 1901 George Cecil reported to *The Accountants' Magazine* about 'The Hindu Accountant'. 'He is careful in his work, exceedingly neat and tidy, and, moreover, he writes a hand of the most admirable copper-plate description'. The Hindu accountant was ubiquitous. 'In the offices and stations of the East India Railway Company he literally swarms. In the brick factories round about Calcutta, as well as in the numerous native flour-mills which adorn the suburbs of the "city of palaces", he shines as an accountant and cashier. In the Government telegraph offices he is responsible for the correctness of the accounts, and in the post-offices he keeps an eye to the receipts'.

Early Days 4: Happiness

David Murray's history of the early days of accounting also records how early accountants were particularly convivial people. He recounts an 1825 account of one James Balfour who was an Edinburgh accountant in the late eighteenth century. 'This remarkable personage was a man of respectable appearance, and had all the manners of a gentleman of the old school. He was, by profession, an accountant; but was more noted as a great singer – a great drinker – a great Jacobite – and a great golfer. Indeed his convivial habits almost completely unfitted him for business; and it was a matter of surprise to some of his acquaintance, how he contrived to live. Yet live he did, and drink, and sing, and make merry, to the last – when no less was the surprise of his friends, upon finding that he left some money'. Another tale was recounted of Balfour:

> *A lady, who lived in Parliament Close, told a friend of mine that she was wakened from her sleep one summer morning by a noise as of singing, when, going to the window to learn what was the matter, guess her surprise at seeing Jamie Balfour and some of his boon companions singing "The King shall enjoy his own again", on their knees, around King Charles's statue.*

But to set records straighter it was also reported that:

> *Report speaks of this person as an amiable, upright, and able man; so clever in his business matters that he could do as much in one hour as another man in three; always eager to quench and arrest litigation rather than to promote it; and consequently so much esteemed professionally, that he could get business whenever he chose to undertake it, which, however he only did when he felt himself in need of money.*

The Emergence and Consolidation of the Chartered Accountancy Profession in Scotland

BY

Stephen P Walker

Lord Palmerston, the Home Secretary, signed the Royal Warrant for the incorporation of The Society of Accountants in Edinburgh on 23 October 1854. On that day a correspondent of *The Times* wrote:

> *That it is the principal subject of conversation in London and Paris is a matter of course; in the highlands of Scotland and through the tourist's beaten track in continental Europe Englishmen will be discussing continually the great event and its consequences.*

Alas this was no reference to the award of a Royal Charter to a small community of professional men in the capital of Scotland. Popular attention was focused on more pressing events elsewhere. During the autumn of 1854 the news was dominated by the war in the Crimea.

On 28 March Britain and France had declared war on Russia. In September 60,000 allied troops invaded the Crimean Peninsula with the object of capturing Sebastopol and destroying the Russian fleet. On 23 October 1853 the press reported that while there was every prospect of military success, the suffering of British casualties was appalling. Hundreds of sick and wounded lay unattended in the military hospital at Scutari. More men were lost to cholera than enemy action. On 21 October Florence Nightingale and 34 nurses had left for the war zone. Four days later one the most disastrous episodes in modern British military history took place, the suicidal Charge of the Light Brigade. Hence, for contemporaries the award of a Royal Charter to a Society of Accountants in Edinburgh was an event of small moment. It was, however, a landmark in the history of a profession which was to assume a major role in the modern age. The object of this article is to narrate the events which culminated in the formation of the first institutes of accountants in Edinburgh and Glasgow in 1853, their achievement of royal charters in 1854 and 1855 and the creation of ICAS nearly a century later in 1951.

The causes of the formation of the organisations of professional accountants in Scotland in 1853 have been a source of controversy among accounting historians. The subject has attracted much attention. This is not merely due to curiosity about the origins of the accountancy profession but because the pattern of professional organisation established in Edinburgh, Glasgow, and later in Aberdeen, was subsequently emulated elsewhere. The local city-based professional bodies in Scotland were mirrored by most of the organisations that merged as the ICAEW in 1880 (in Liverpool and London (1870), Manchester (1871) and Sheffield (1877)). The Scottish institutes also established the principles that membership be confined to public practitioners, and that incorporation by royal charter and the designation 'chartered accountant' were the desirable forms of public recognition for professional accountants. These geographical and work-based criteria for entry established the character of accounting professionalism. However, their narrowness also set the scene for the later proliferation of accountancy bodies in the British Isles.

Explanations for early professional organisation in Scotland

Students of the formation of the institutes of accountants in Edinburgh and Glasgow in 1853 have focused on three possible explanations for professional organisation. Firstly, early professionalisation in Scotland is perceived as a consequence of the different legal systems of England and Scotland, particularly the law of bankruptcy. Secondly, organisation was a result of the emergence of an urban-industrial society and increased demand for accounting services. Thirdly, professional formation in Scotland was induced by the need for established accountancy practitioners to close the profession to outsiders, achieve a distinctive identity and improve their social status. Some observers have been noticeably circumspect on the subject of causes. One commentator asserted:

the movement was entirely spontaneous. There was no legislative pressure nor even any official encouragement.

More recent research has suggested that this was far from the case. Accounting historians increasingly recognise that the circumstances surrounding the organisation of professional groups is invariably complex and specific to time and place. Therefore, to capture the story of the organisation of accountants in Edinburgh and Glasgow in 1853 it is necessary to understand the socio-economic and political context in which practitioners decided to form a professional body and seek its recognition by the state.

It is important to establish that Edinburgh accountants were a highly respected group long before they formed an institute in 1853. By the end of the eighteenth century there were almost 40 accountants in Scotland, concentrated in Edinburgh and Glasgow. Half a century later there were over 300. The eminent Scots lawyer Bell stated in 1826:

… in this country we have a set of professional accountants, possessing a degree of intelligence, and a respectability of character, scarcely equalled in any unincorporated body of professional men.

Public accountants in early nineteenth century Edinburgh were seen as equal in status to solicitors. It was when this status was threatened that accountants in the major Scottish cities were motivated to protect themselves through organisation. In fact, the bodies formed in 1853 and chartered in 1854 and 1855 were not the first organisations of Scottish accountants. In 1834 a group of Edinburgh accountants formed a Committee of Accountants Practising Before the Court of Session (chaired by James Brown, who later became the first President of the Society of Accountants in Edinburgh) as a pressure group to protect their work as auditors of judicial factories. These audit appointments were threatened by legislative proposals. This reason for organisation, joining together to protect economic interests, resonates strongly with the circumstances leading to the creation of more enduring professional bodies in 1853.

A threat from the south, 1852-1853

From a modern-day perspective it is difficult to perceive the significance of bankruptcy to the Victorians. The subject was not only important to the operation of commerce; it was a wider social and moral concern. The workings of the laws of bankruptcy and insolvency were the subject of numerous bills, royal commissions, and parliamentary committees during the nineteenth century. Those who examine the early minute books of the Edinburgh and Glasgow institutes cannot fail to notice the frequent reference to bankruptcy legislation. This reflects the fact that bankruptcy and insolvency administration were major sources of fee income for practitioners. Traditionally, historians have focused on the importance of formal bankruptcy to public accountants in Scotland. We now know that accountants were also heavily engaged in the winding-up of insolvent estates under voluntary trusts. The fact that the laws and processes of bankruptcy and insolvency were distinctive in Scotland provides the backdrop to the early organisation of accountants north of the border in 1853.

Defects in the system of administering insolvent estates in Scotland were discussed frequently during the early 1850s. From this debate emerged proposals that posed a massive threat to the practice of public accountants north of the border. The menace was the Bankruptcy and Insolvency (Scotland) Bill, 1853. Accountants in Edinburgh and Glasgow established protective organisations to prevent this offensive measure from entering the statute book. In order to understand the threat posed by this bill, it is necessary to explore the context in which it emerged and the motives and influence of its sponsors.

In 1851 a group of London warehousemen trading with Scotland formed the 'London Committee of Merchants and Others Associated for the Improvement of the Commercial and Bankruptcy Laws of Scotland, and the Assimilation of Those Laws in England and Scotland'. By September 1852 the London Committee comprised 22 merchants, four Liberal MPs and six lawyers. The Committee had formed as a result of its members feeling aggrieved at incurring heavy losses as creditors of a Glasgow bankrupt. The London Committee made extensive inquiries into the working of the law of bankruptcy in Scotland and in October 1852 produced a *Report and Suggestions Addressed to the Mercantile Community of the United Kingdom*. This report listed a number of evils. The principal grievance was the Scottish system of vesting the management of the bankrupt's estate in the hands of a trustee and paying him 'exorbitant' levels of commission out of the bankrupt's estate. Moreover, the London Committee complained that many trustees were insufficiently qualified for their appointed task. The group who most commonly held the position of trustee was accountants. The London Committee proposed to remedy the defects of the Scottish system of insolvency by imposing the English process of bankruptcy on Scotland. So far as the accountants of Edinburgh and Glasgow were concerned this would mean that remunerative sequestration trusteeships would be lost and transferred to a small number of judicial officers. Further, the hitherto unregulated and lucrative system of voluntary trusteeships enjoyed by Scottish accountants would be placed under the supervision and scrutiny of the courts.

The unorganised accountants of Scotland had every reason to fear that the London Committee's campaign to reform the Scots law of bankruptcy would be successful. Among the London Committee's members were some of the most significant businessmen in the capital. In addition, the London Committee zealously mobilised the support of the influential mercantile, manufacturing and legal communities. Public meetings, lecture tours and personal lobbying were planned to highlight the national importance of the issue. *The Trade Protection Circular* warned that:

> ... *these men have power ... [and] they are using it unscrupulously to excite an electoral opinion, and a consequent parliamentary influence, in England, which, if not met and counteracted, will enable them to carry all their day-dreams and extravagances into effect.*

In order to achieve the overhaul of the Scottish bankruptcy law, the London Committee commissioned its Secretary to draft a bill for consideration by Parliament.

In order to cultivate wide support the London Committee's reforms were also advanced on the basis of dominant philosophies of the day: free trade and the assimilation of commercial law. Free trade was the prevailing economic doctrine of the mid-nineteenth century. It embraced more than a crusade for the removal of restraints on the exchange of goods. Free trade was perceived as a means of binding nations and reducing international conflict. One impediment to achieving these ideals was the conflicting nature of the commercial laws of countries engaging in free trade. The solution was the 'assimilation' or homogenisation of the commercial laws of nations.

Demands for the assimilation of law were made during the late 1840s and early 1850s. Britain's domination of world trade encouraged interest in the development of international codes of commerce. It was assumed that standardised laws on subjects such as contract, bills of exchange and bankruptcy would improve the circulation of capital and encourage the development of international business and goodwill. These ideas were also to the fore during an event of considerable significance in Victorian Britain, that testament to industrial progress, the Great Exhibition of 1851. While the objective of unifying the commercial laws of all nations was considered by many to be unattainable, others perceived that a realistic starting point would be to assimilate the separate mercantile laws of England, Scotland and Ireland and thereby extend commercial relations within the British Isles. One area identified by advocates of assimilation as deserving attention was the law of bankruptcy. The London Committee advanced free trade and assimilation arguments in support of its proposals to impose the English law of bankruptcy and insolvency on Scotland. It argued that the bankruptcy law of Scotland was an impediment to the internal trade of Britain.

By the autumn of 1852 a number of developments showed Scottish accountants that the threat posed by the London Committee and its proposed reforms was extremely serious. In November a major conference took place in London on the assimilation of the mercantile laws of England, Scotland and Ireland. The conference sent a deputation to the Prime Minister, the Earl of Derby, who expressed support for assimilation. On 16 December 1852 there was a change of government. The new Prime Minister, the Earl of Aberdeen, stated that his government would pursue policies of free trade and law reform.

The initial response of leading Edinburgh accountants to the threat of bankruptcy law reform from London was to publish a series of pamphlets. The first and most influential of these was *Reform of the Bankruptcy Law of Scotland* by Samuel Raleigh. This appeared at the end of 1852. Raleigh, whose role in the organisation of the profession in Edinburgh has been scantily acknowledged in histories of ICAS, rebutted the London Committee's allegations about the defects of the

Scottish law of bankruptcy. However, he did recognise that the London Committee's concerns about the qualifications of trustees had some validity. Although Raleigh showed that 75% of bankrupt estates in Scotland were managed by 'professional trustees' (of whom the majority were accountants), he conceded the need to exclude incompetent men from these appointments. Raleigh suggested that this might be achieved by restricting the selection of trustees from those named on public certified lists of suitably qualified individuals These qualified trustees might also be organised "as a separate professional body". Raleigh's ideas were supported by a group of Edinburgh accountants who, in another pamphlet, *Remarks on The Revision of the Bankruptcy Laws of Scotland*, 1853, also rejected the London Committee's proposals. Raleigh's suggestion of organising a qualified body of trustees as a professional body was considered 'highly beneficial'. The pamphleteers also argued that if the law of bankruptcy was to be reformed, the agenda should be set in Edinburgh, not London.

The Institutes of Accountants in Edinburgh and Glasgow, 1853

It was in the context of the imminent threat to their bankruptcy and insolvency practice and demands for the organisation of qualified trustees that the first move was made on 17 January 1853 to "bring about some definite arrangement for uniting the professional Accountants in Edinburgh". The minute books of the Institute of Accountants in Edinburgh reveal that the need to organise was pressing. By 22 January 1853 a draft constitution was discussed and attempts were made to enrol suitable members "with as little delay as possible". Why this urgency? The London Committee's promised Bill to overhaul the Scottish system of bankruptcy administration and replace it with the English system was now drafted. The offending Bankruptcy and Insolvency (Scotland) Bill proposed that the management of bankrupt estates would be vested in five Official Assignees for Scotland rather than in the 862 trusteeships currently filled by accountants (60%), lawyers (10%), bankers (4%), merchants and others (26%). Voluntary trusts for behoof of creditors – a highly lucrative source of income for accountants and lawyers - were to be supervised by new Courts of Bankruptcy and Insolvency. On the same day that the Institute of Accountants discussed its constitution, the chairman of the London Committee was in Edinburgh to explain the merits of the Bankruptcy and Insolvency (Scotland) Bill to the local chamber of commerce.

In early 1853 it appeared that there was every prospect of the offending Bankruptcy and Insolvency (Scotland) Bill becoming law. The London Committee claimed that the government received the Bill "in a friendly manner". The parliamentary sponsor of the Bill was Henry, Lord Brougham, a powerful political figure in the 1850s. The Bankruptcy and Insolvency (Scotland) Bill received its First Reading in the House of Lords on 15 March 1853. Its appearance galvanised an alliance of accountants, lawyers and merchants in Edinburgh into vigorous lobbying of the principal government representative in Scotland - the Lord Advocate, James Moncreiff, whose son was among the founding members of the Institute of Accountants in Edinburgh. The result was the introduction to the House of Commons on 4 May 1853 of an alternative measure to the London Committee's Bill, the Bankruptcy (Scotland) Bill. This, the Lord Advocate's Bill, contained a mere 18 clauses designed to remedy the most obvious defects of Scottish bankruptcy administration and thereby negate the need for the radical reforms proposed by the London Committee.

However, the appearance of the Bankruptcy (Scotland) Bill did not quell the activism of the London Committee. In fact it encouraged renewed lobbying. Petitions in favour of the London Committee's Bankruptcy and Insolvency (Scotland) Bill were signed by over 200 merchants in London. The Bill passed its Second Reading in the House of Lords on 22 July 1853. The Lord Advocate's Bankruptcy

(Scotland) Bill was passed in August with little parliamentary discussion. The London Committee considered that the Lord Advocate's measure was totally inadequate and redoubled its efforts to secure more radical legislation. The Committee prepared a *Second Address to the Mercantile Community of the United Kingdom*, which was widely circulated during the summer of 1853 to encourage the petitioning of Parliament against the system of insolvency administration in Scotland. The Secretary of the London Committee was sent on a campaign to lobby mercantile and legal organisations in the major commercial and manufacturing centres of Britain. The 'second city of the Empire' was singled out for particular attention.

If the London Committee was to find a sympathetic ear in Scotland it was likely to find it in Glasgow. Many Glaswegian merchants and industrialists supported assimilationist measures designed to enhance trade with England. Some Glasgow lawyers were also sympathetic to reforms which reduced the power of the legal establishment in Edinburgh. Hence, the London Committee's proposals were looked upon favourably by organisations such as the Glasgow Law Amendment Society and the Glasgow and West of Scotland Society for the Protection of Trade. Until the autumn of 1853 agitation against the London Committee's Bill was Edinburgh-centred. In late September 1853 further parliamentary discussion of the bankruptcy laws of Scotland seemed inevitable. A public meeting was organised by the London Committee in Glasgow for October to discuss its Bankruptcy and Insolvency (Scotland) Bill. Like their brethren in Edinburgh the accountants of Glasgow needed to organise to protect their interests in bankruptcy and insolvency work.

Hence, in September 1853 27 accountants who commenced practice after 1841 requisitioned their more senior colleagues to consider the formation of an organisation of professional practitioners in Glasgow. The requisition stated that organisation was necessary because of "the late changes and contemplated alterations in the Bankrupt Law of Scotland", and "in order that the practical experience of those parties who have hitherto been entrusted with the management of Bankrupt Estates in the West of Scotland may be properly represented, and have due weight in determining what changes require to be made upon the existing Bankrupt Law". The Institute of Accountants and Actuaries in Glasgow was formed on 3 October 1853.

Two to three hundred persons attended the "great" public meeting in Glasgow to discuss the London Committee's Bankruptcy and Insolvency (Scotland) Bill in late October 1853. One of the founders of the new Institute of Accountants in Glasgow made a vigorous defence of the existing system of bankruptcy administration in Scotland. However, like Raleigh he conceded that it "is an evil in our current system, and a great one too, that any man, whatever may be his abilities or qualifications, may be elected trustee". A solution would be to prepare a certified list of experienced trustees eligible for election, presumably the members of an institute of accountants in Glasgow.

Accountants and nationalism

It was stated earlier that the threat of the London Committee was rendered especially potent by the enlistment of powerful arguments founded on free trade and assimilation. This demanded that Scottish accountants offered compelling counter-arguments in support of their efforts to retain the existing laws of insolvency and bankruptcy and repel the demands of the London Committee. The accountants reverted to the seductive appeal of nationalism - an ideology that was to be mobilised during later episodes when the position of practitioners in Scotland was uncertain, such as the proposal to create an Institute of Chartered Accountants of Great Britain in 1989.

The period when institutes were formed in Edinburgh and Glasgow was one of emerging Scottish nationalism. These sentiments were aroused by English dominance of the machinery of government and the increasing provincialisation of Scotland. Attempts to assimilate the laws of Scotland with those of England were signs of creeping Anglicisation and aroused discontent, particularly in Edinburgh. In May 1853 a National Association for the Vindication of Scottish Rights was formed and by November of the same year boasted 6,000 members. The National Association argued for the preservation of the national laws and institutions of Scotland. Among its supporters were those directly threatened by assimilation measures from London – accountants. The membership lists of the General Committee of the National Association included the names of five accountants. The secretaries of the Edinburgh and Glasgow branches of the National Association for the Vindication of Scottish Rights were accountants and "leading spirits" of the movement. Another accountant, Robert Christie senior, wrote a scathing pamphlet on the inequitable distribution of government expenditure between England and Scotland.

The accountants who authored pamphlets on the law of insolvency in 1852–1853 expressed considerable resentment at the attempted imposition of the English system of bankruptcy administration on Scotland. Samuel Raleigh argued that the assimilation of the bankruptcy laws ignored the indigenous legal system and the nature of Scottish society. He argued:

> *Let us remember that the Scottish character has tendencies and peculiarities of its own, which will not readily accommodate themselves to imported methods and foreign systems of procedure.*

Raleigh objected to the "violent and wholesale substitution" of the Scottish system of bankruptcy by the English, and was offended that demands for change had emanated from London. He urged action to devise reforms that would "save the country from rash and ill-advised experiments". Another original member of the Edinburgh Institute, Christopher Douglas, argued that although in many respects England

and Scotland were a single country, on the law of bankruptcy "no two countries scarcely can bear less resemblance to each other". Despite the Union of 1707 Scotland retained "a determined love of her own independent laws" and its people were firmly resolved not to have unsuitable 'foreign' English jurisprudence thrust upon them.

The nationalist ideology became a rallying call to other groups such as merchants and lawyers who (as trustees) had a direct interest in the maintenance of the Scottish bankruptcy procedure. The result was the emergence of a coalition of accountants and other groups that fought the London Committee's proposals. For example, the Edinburgh Chamber of Commerce objected that the London Committee was attempting to make Scotland "a sort of experimental garden of legislation for England, on a bill prepared by English parties". Samuel Raleigh argued that interested parties in Scotland, not Londoners, should devise their own proposals for bankruptcy reform. The result was The Edinburgh General Committee on Bankruptcy Law Reform that met on 18 February 1853. The General Committee immediately appointed a 34 man sub-committee (chaired by Raleigh) containing bankers, merchants, lawyers and four accountants (who were particularly active in the affairs of the early Edinburgh Institute) to investigate the bankruptcy laws in Scotland and to watch measures brought into Parliament on the subject. The General Committee resolved that the fundamentals of the Scots law of bankruptcy were sound, that reform should have "due regard to the working of our own legal principles and institutions" and that trusteeships should be confined to qualified professionals whose names appeared on certified lists. This appeal to patriotism also enlisted the support of Scottish MPs and policy-makers, the most important of whom was the Lord Advocate, James Moncreiff. The result was the subsequent widespread condemnation of the London Committee's bankruptcy and insolvency bill in Scotland.

Having received the support of the Lord Advocate and interested public opinion, the coalition of professional and commercial groups in Scotland were ready to confront the re-introduction of the London Committee's Bill in the House of Lords on 10 March 1854. Sixteen petitions were presented from Scotland of which only one was in favour of the Bill. Although the measure passed its Second Reading in the Lords in April 1854, the weight of Scottish opposition and the lukewarm response of the government ensured that it proceeded no further in 1854. The subsequent progress of the London Committee's Bill was effectively scuppered by the Lord Advocate who, later in 1854, requested the Faculty of Advocates to prepare a report on the Scots bankruptcy laws. The resulting report was the precursor to the Bankruptcy (Scotland) Act, 1856, which remained the primary insolvency statute north of the border until 1913.

There is an ironic twist to this story. Although the London Committee failed to impose the English law of bankruptcy on Scotland during the 1850s, assimilation was temporarily achieved in the period 1870-1883, not by the imposition of English laws on Scotland but by the adoption of Scottish insolvency practice in England *via* the Bankruptcy Act, 1869. By the 1860s it was recognised that the Scottish process of bankruptcy administration was more efficient and effective than the officialist system in England and Wales. The appointment of professional accountants to manage insolvent estates in Scotland was deemed worthy of emulation south of the border. The Attorney General expressed the hope that the effect of introducing the Scottish system of creditor-elected trustees would "be to create a similar profession" of accountant trustees in England. When the Bankruptcy Act, 1869 was passed trusteeships were open to anyone who wished to compete for them. The need to determine a division of labour between accountants and solicitors in bankruptcy administration and the threat to established accountants of a "herd of disreputable persons" seeking trusteeships, encouraged the formation of local societies of accountants in Liverpool and London in 1870 when the new Bankruptcy Act came into force.

The Charters, 1854-1855

The evidence suggests that the initial object in forming professional bodies in Edinburgh and Glasgow was the creation of protective organisations geared for political contest and the preservation of collective interests in insolvency work. The establishment of qualifying associations was a secondary objective. Hence, when the Edinburgh Institute revealed its first constitution it was chastised for the absence of provisions relating to fundamental subjects such as the education and qualification of members. The constitution was criticised as "hastily and crudely concocted". Once the challenge to insolvency work had abated the Institute of Accountants in Edinburgh could turn its attention to measures for creating an enduring qualifying association. Foremost among these measures was seeking state recognition through a Royal Charter of incorporation. The chairman of the first meetings of the Institute of Accountants in Edinburgh, Archibald Borthwick (Samuel Raleigh's partner), stated on 31 January 1853 that application for a Royal Charter was an ultimate objective. At the first annual meeting of the Institute on 1 February 1854 the time was considered ripe for pursuing this aim and on 30 May the members of the Institute approved a draft petition for the incorporation of a Society of Accountants in Edinburgh. Interestingly, the latter meeting appears to have been convened according to a timescale that was *ultra vires* the rules of the Institute. Haste was the result of an attempt to take advantage of the imminent departure of the Institute's solicitor for London where the case for a royal charter might be pursued.

The path to achieving the first Royal Charter was not particularly smooth. One complication was the existence of two classes of membership of the Institute of Accountants in Edinburgh – 'ordinary members' (who were practising accountants) and 'honorary members' (who formerly practised as accountants but now held other appointments, such as manager of a life assurance company or officer of the court).

The charter petition concerned practising public accountants and not those engaged in other occupations. Hence, honorary members either resigned from the Institute or became ordinary members. Sixty-one members eventually signed the charter petition.

The Society of Solicitors to the Supreme Court was also anxious that the charter would not confer exclusive privileges on accountants to the detriment of its own members, and, in particular, a monopoly of remits from the Court of Session. The Society also argued that the accountants should ensure that provision be made for the education of apprentices prior to admission. On 4 October 1854 the Society wrote to the Lord Advocate to express its concern that the charter "may contain powers which may interfere with, and be prejudicial to, the rights and interests of the Members". In November the Society decided to petition the Privy Council and asked the Lord Advocate to see the draft charter before the matter was further proceeded with. While the solicitors thought it desirable that Edinburgh accountants be incorporated their Society was angered to discover that by the time its petition reached London, the charter had already been granted. Notice of the application for the charter had only been made once in *The London Gazette* instead of the usual three times in both the *London* and *Edinburgh Gazettes*. The Society of Solicitors to the Supreme Court complained to the Lord Advocate that it should have been consulted about the accountants' charter and that its officers had not been "treated in the way they had a right to expect". A deputation from the Society met the Lord Advocate in late November and was assured that the charter petition did not contain provisions that would interfere with solicitors. The Lord Advocate also expressed regret at his failure to consult the Society. Following this meeting the concerns of the solicitors were allayed.

Another issue arose from the fact that the members of the Institute of Accountants who petitioned for the charter represented only half the accountants in Edinburgh. Not all practitioners excluded from the petition accepted this without complaint. On 17 August 1854 William Myrtle and seven other accountants in Edinburgh sent a memorial on the charter petition to the Privy Council in London. When the Lord Advocate was asked by the Board of Trade to offer his opinion on the charter application he expressed support but failed to interview the excluded memorialists. Three discontented memorialists, D Murray, J Moinet and W Myrtle, complained that their right to be heard had been violated. In September Myrtle also enlisted the support of the MP for the City of Edinburgh. The Lord Advocate met with four of the disenchanted accountants on 5 October and informed them that a fair way to determine membership of the new Society of Accountants in Edinburgh would be to include those listed as accountants in the *Edinburgh Almanac*. Myrtle also received a letter from Samuel Raleigh on 10 October advising him that his opposition to the charter was unnecessary because he would certainly be admitted to the Society once the charter was granted. However, on 14 December 1854 Myrtle discovered that a certified list of members prepared by the Secretary of the Institute of Accountants excluded his name and those of other memorialists. Murray and Moinet had been included on the Lord Advocate's recommendation. Myrtle assumed that members of the Institute had decided that he was not an accountant and therefore excluded him. He argued that some of those named in the petition for the charter had less right than he to be included as 'accountants'. Myrtle was so aggrieved that on 18 December he threatened the Lord Advocate with further action:

> …*[if] your Lordship now refuses to see justice done to me I shall not only publish a series of letters in all the Edinburgh Newspapers but cause the Charter Memorial, correspondence and Strictures thereon to be printed and circulated among the Members of the Legal Profession, Chamber of Commerce &c in Edinburgh and all the Members of the House of Commons preparatory to bringing the case before Parliament.*

*As I can count on the support of many leading English Members
and most of the Scotch Members I am determined to have the whole
business thoroughly exposed … I am resolved to obtain justice by
appealing to Parliament if justice is not now awarded to me.*

Moinet, Murray and Myrtle were formally admitted to the
Society of Accountants in Edinburgh on 29 December 1854 on the
Lord Advocate's recommendation. At this general meeting the newly
incorporated Society was formally established. On 30 January 1855
it was resolved that members would add the abbreviation 'CA' after
their names.

The pursuit of a Royal Charter by the Institute of Accountants and
Actuaries in Glasgow appears to have been less fraught. The council
of the Institute was scheduled to discuss the matter on 17 May 1854,
before the Edinburgh petition was approved, but the meeting was
inquorate. On 4 July the council decided to take the necessary steps
to prepare an application, considering that a charter "would greatly
improve the position of the Institute, and promote the objectives it
had in view". On 6 July a special general meeting resolved to pursue
an application "as soon as practicable". On 18 August a draft petition
and charter was discussed and it was decided not to await the outcome
of the application for a charter by the Edinburgh Institute. There was
some disagreement over the title of the proposed chartered body –
whether it should be the Institute of Accountants in Glasgow or the
Institute of Accountants and Actuaries in Glasgow. In fact, although
most members of the Institute were involved in insurance agency, very
few were actuaries. The title Institute of Accountants and Actuaries
in Glasgow was agreed on 24 August 1854. Forty-nine members of
the Institute, who represented only one-third of the accountants in
Glasgow, signed a petition in September. The Royal Warrant was
granted on 15 March 1855. A Society of Accountants in Aberdeen
was founded by twelve practitioners in 1866 and a Royal Charter
granted on 18 March 1867.

Formation of The Institute of Chartered Accountants of Scotland, 1951

A distinctive feature of the history of the accountancy profession in Scotland is its organisation, for almost a century, on a local basis. In England, by contrast, the city-based societies that formed during the 1870s in Liverpool, London, Manchester and Sheffield had merged as a national institute by 1880. This points to the distinctive identities of accountants in the east and west of Scotland.

Studies of the founders of the institutes in 1853 indicate that accountants in Edinburgh and Glasgow were cohesive, but based on quite different sets of relationships. Edinburgh accountants were associated with landed society, lawyers and actuaries. Glasgow accountants were associated with the commercial, manufacturing and trading communities. These differences were reflected in the clientele of accountants in the two cities. Edinburgh accountants were accorded a lofty status on the basis of their association with the landed interest and the legal profession. These connections were founded on kinship ties, business associations and social contacts made through church and membership of local organisations. Their association with commerce meant that accountants in Glasgow were accorded a lower status, at least outside of the west of Scotland. In 1896 James Martin (not the most impartial of observers) concluded:

> I do not know whether it is the case that in Glasgow we have a lower type of CA than exists elsewhere. If I did say so I should not be the first to record the observation.

A major source of difference between Edinburgh and Glasgow accountants was the involvement of many Glasgow accountants in stockbroking. This association persisted in some degree until the 1940s. Twelve of the first sixteen chairmen of the Glasgow Stock Exchange were members of the Institute of Accountants and Actuaries in Glasgow.

Half of the Institute's founders were also members of the local stock exchange. In 1870 membership of the Glasgow Institute is reputed to have comprised 37 stockbrokers, 27 accountants and no actuaries. For Edinburgh accountants the receipt of brokerage commission was alien to notions of the independent public practitioner.

Differences between accountants in the east and west were also reflected in the sources of recruits. Recruitment to the Edinburgh Society during the nineteenth century reflected the connections between Edinburgh accountants, the professional class and the landed interest. In Glasgow a higher proportion of CAs emanated from families in commerce, manufacturing and trade. There were also differences in the policies pursued by the organisations in the east and west. Disagreements arose, for example, over proposals for the amalgamation of the three societies during the late nineteenth and early twentieth centuries (these were opposed in Edinburgh). The Edinburgh Society was much more elitist in recruitment, imposing an apprenticeship fee of 100 guineas for a five year indenture and an admission fee of the same amount during the 1880s. The Glasgow Institute considered itself more meritocratic and perceived apprenticeship fees as an impediment to the social mobility of local youths. Further, the period of indentures in Glasgow was four years and the admission fee was half that charged in Edinburgh. These divergences resulted in periodic tensions between the Edinburgh Society and the Glasgow Institute on a number of issues that were played out in the context of a shift in the distribution of power between east and west. The Edinburgh Society was numerically dominant until 1902 and had greater prestige. However, the membership of the Glasgow Institute expanded rapidly during the early twentieth century and by 1950 was 2.5 times larger than the Edinburgh Society and 14 times larger than the Society of Accountants in Aberdeen.

Despite their differences the CAs of Edinburgh and Glasgow found common cause when their collective interests were under threat, as in 1854 over bankruptcy legislation. Attempts by rival bodies such as the Scottish Institute of Accountants (formed in 1880) and the Corporation of Accountants (1891) to usurp the privileges of the Edinburgh, Glasgow and Aberdeen societies were the backdrop to consideration of the formation of an amalgamated national organisation of chartered accountants in Scotland during the late nineteenth century. These proposals came to nought due to reluctance in Edinburgh. However, incremental moves towards greater co-operation were taken, particularly during the 1890s. These included devising a common scheme of examinations (1892-1951), the establishment of a joint committee (from 1894) and a formal Joint Committee of Councils (from 1915) to discuss matters of mutual concern, the collective pursuit of registration bills (1896-1898), the appearance of a professional journal (*The Accountants' Magazine*, from 1897) and the invention of the title 'Scottish Chartered Accountants' (in 1896-7).

As was revealed in 1852-1853 when the London Committee of Merchants sought reforms antagonistic to their interests, Scottish CAs have periodically been galvanised into united responses to external threats that have emanated from London. Suspicions have been easily aroused in Scotland about London proposals for structural changes to the profession. The ICAEW became the dominant force from 1880 and the main engine house of plans to rationalise the profession. The ICAEW faced greater competition from non-chartered accountants in its own backyard than was the case in Scotland. Scottish CAs have often objected to the need for change and the manner in which proposals from England for rationalisation have been insensitive to concerns north of the border.

It was as a result of plans to co-ordinate the British accountancy profession during the 1940s that the bodies in Edinburgh, Glasgow and Aberdeen eventually merged as ICAS in 1951. In 1930 there were at least 17 organisations of accountants in the British Isles. Several attempts to integrate the accountancy bodies and secure the closure of the profession by registration ensued. From 1942 an effort was made to co-ordinate the accountancy profession and secure the statutory licensing of public accountants. This, ultimately unsuccessful venture was ICAEW-led and London centred. The negotiations revealed that the representation of Scottish interests through the Joint Committee of Councils and three professional organisations was cumbersome. In December 1943 the council of the Glasgow Institute called for the amalgamation of the Edinburgh, Glasgow and Aberdeen societies. However, it was decided not to take the matter further until the war was over. The issue was re-ignited at the end of 1945 by a group of young, radical CAs in Glasgow. As a result, Sir David Allen Hay, President of the Glasgow Institute, proposed to the Joint Committee of Councils that amalgamation be discussed. A sub-committee of the Joint Committee was established in 1945 to consider the matter. The centenary history of ICAS referred to numerous difficulties and the 'glacial speed' towards unification that ensued. The Edinburgh Society was reluctant to surrender the oldest charter in the accountancy profession. There were also debates about whether a unified institute should be based in Edinburgh or Glasgow (or both). Complications arose over the status of the Endowment and Annuity Fund of the Edinburgh Society. When the merger proposals were finally put to the members, unanimous approval was secured in Edinburgh and Aberdeen. Gaining a majority of Glasgow members proved more difficult, though this was eventually achieved.

The charters of the Institute of Accountants and Actuaries in Glasgow and the Society of Accountants in Aberdeen were surrendered and the members of these organisations joined the Society of Accountants in Edinburgh, which was reconstituted as The Institute of Chartered Accountants of Scotland under a supplemental charter. A major player in this event, Sir David Allen Hay, commented that the merger would:

... enable the Scottish Chartered Accountants as a unified body, to take a more effective place in their association with the other bodies of organised accountants in Great Britain than has been possible hitherto.

This proved to be the case over the next half century.

Stephen Walker is Professor of Accounting at Cardiff University. He is editor of *The Accounting Historians Journal* and has authored a number of articles and books on the history of the accountancy profession. He was Convener of the Scottish Committee on Accounting History of ICAS and is currently a member of the Research Committee.

Early Days 5: Nae Auditing

Sir John Mann CA, celebrated the Centenary of the Institute in 1954 by recalling both his experiences and those of his father before him. He had lost all his money in the great collapse of the City of Glasgow Bank but recovered to become President of the Glasgow Institute in the year after it celebrated its fifty years of existence in 1905. Looking back to the early nineteenth century Sir John said that:

> *the most striking impression I have formed of the work done by the early accountants is that it was an extraordinary medley – what they probably called in their Lallans dialect a kind of clamjamfry or gallimaufry. There was plenty of accounting work, writing up and balancing books, preparing accounts, but strangely not a trace of auditing.*

Scots Outwith 3: Dyspepsia

In January 1903 George Cecil was reporting on the life of the expatriate accountant. He was not enthusiastic. 'The social life of the bank or mercantile accountant is often a weariness to the flesh. In a word, it may be his misfortune to be bored to death'. Even other expatriates did not cheer him. 'In the event of his fellow exiles being intensely uninteresting, and, consequently, extremely boring, their presence will avail the accountant naught. Thus, should he be unable to take any pleasure in their society, he will be forced to spend his leisure in reading and writing, unless he cares to bicycle, golf, or ride by himself. Shooting and pig-sticking is at his disposal – should he be fortunate in being stationed in a district in which sport of this nature is obtainable'. Even the standby of the Empire, the club, didn't cheer him. 'It should be borne in mind that ladies are also admitted to Anglo-Indian clubs', he reports. 'But, even with this inducement thrown in, the accountant is apt to find an hour or so at the club a very poor form of amusement'. He even disparages the drinking habits. 'On first joining an Indian club', he says, 'the newly-arrived accountant will be somewhat astonished at the amount of whiskies-and-sodas and liqueurs disposed of by the members between tea and dinner-time; for it appears to be a recognised custom to ask his friends to "have a drink" directly a member accosts them. And the expatriated man of mathematics wonders that he suffers from premature liver complaint ...'. The climate has got to him as well. Cecil reports that:

In fact on the plains of India, wherever one happens to be living during the summer and autumn months, one is certain to be in a disgusting state of perspiration for the greater part of the twenty-four hours. In spite, however, of these drawbacks the exiled accountant takes kindly to cricket and football – however hot it may be.

He perks up at the climate of Simla but in the end his dyspepsia gets the better of him. He concludes his report:

It may therefore be repeated that the emigrant railway, commercial, or bank accountant is frequently bored by the relaxations placed at his disposal.

Early Days 6: Nae Dinner

Sir John Mann, in his reminiscences in 1954, drew on the experiences of his father before him. In his apprenticeship in 1842–1847 he had worked in 'small, homely, rather dingy "counting-houses" as they were then called – equipped with high sloping desks and high

backless stools. The partners and the staff lived near their work, the
"governor" sometimes in the same buildings as the office, so that
no time was lost in travelling; getting home for meals was easy. This
explains why business hours were from 10 till 4, then two hours
break, and work again from 6 till 8 and every Saturday till 2. There
were no football matches then, although no doubt urgent funerals to
attend'. Sir John could only trace one radical change in office working
conditions when he himself became an apprentice in 1880, 'when I
climbed on to an old high stool and swung the old copying press'. This
was the abandonment of the two hours dinner break from 4 to 6 pm
and the adoption of a 9 am to 5 pm working day, with Saturday till
2 pm. This probably happened about 1862 when the office was moved
from the noisy city, (153 Queen Street), to what had been a private
dwelling-house in the quiet West End, (983 West Regent Street) – 'a
venture of which my father claimed he had been the pioneer'.

Sundries 1: Winter Evenings

The Scottish Society of Economists met at 8.15 on Friday evenings
in the Accountants' Hall at 27 Queen Street in Edinburgh through the
winter months of 1905-1906. The first meeting was on the subject of:
'Is Economic Science Dismal?' The last was on the subject: 'Do the
British Working Classes contribute an undue proportion to the Imperial
Revenue?' There is no record of any conclusions reached.

New Fangled 2: Postal Scandals

Sir John Mann, in 1954, provided some very Scottish tips on how
the post was used in the late nineteenth century. 'In contrast to the

heavy postage rates, competition for railway traffic was so keen about that time that the fare between Edinburgh and Glasgow was only 6d., compared to 6s.7d., today, so on occasion it was cheaper to send a junior clerk to deliver by hand important bulky letters'. Who said that the cheap air fares of the early twenty-first century create some odd economic anomalies? It is nothing new. Sir John also revealed that the Scots were ingenious in the face of rising postal rates. 'Postage on mail from abroad was charged on delivery, and it was so heavy that families with relatives abroad planned codes of family news by slightly varying the wording on the address; letters could then be rejected unopened without paying the heavy postage'.

The Distaff Side 1: Our Home

In April 1900 an editorial in *The Accountants' Magazine* provided an overview of where women stood in the profession. It seemed quite alarmed. 'In a recent issue of "Our Home" the accountant's profession is discussed, and an instance is given of a lady who is successfully practising in London as a public accountant. We are not aware of any similar instance in Scotland', is its opening. It then continued: 'But that women consider that the profession is not one which should be exclusively in the hands of men is shown by the fact that some time ago, when the Scottish Accountants' Bill was introduced in the House of Commons, the Bill was objected to by the Scottish Women's Liberal Federation on the ground that no provision was made for the registration of female as well as male accountants. In 1894 we understand that a Society for Promoting the Employment of Women memorialised the Council of the Institute of Chartered Accountants in England and Wales to take whatever steps may be necessary for the admission of women as chartered accountants, but we are not aware of any such steps having been taken. On this question the Tasmanian Institute of Accountants take what was apparently the view of the English Institute, as we notice that the Council of the former Institute recently decided, with reference to an application by a woman to be allowed to present herself for examination, that in their opinion "the time has not yet arrived for sanctioning the admission of females into any of the associated Institutes". In New York, however, the ladies have made more progress, a woman having recently passed the necessary examinations and been admitted to the qualification of C.P.A., (Certified Public Accountant)'.

Haggis reaches London

The annual London dinner of the Scots accountants has always been a robust social event to underline the strength of the Scottish accountancy community in London. At one recent dinner the then Lord Chancellor, Lord Mackay of Clashfern, made the point that only ICAS could have dreamt up a structure which referred to England and Wales as merely 'a region'. The dinner was instituted back in the very late nineteenth century. But calamity befell the third. Members learned that: 'The dinner previously arranged for in January last had unfortunately to be abandoned at the last moment owing to the lamented death of Queen Victoria'. But in early December 1901, when it was rearranged, it went with the full swing by which it has been characterised ever since. 'It may not be out of place to add', suggested the report, 'that the essentially Scottish character of the gathering was maintained by an item in the menu which must have been new to many of the guests – haggis to the accompaniment of bagpipes', which doubtless helped the digestion. The same report also underlined the far from hidden agenda of the London annual dinner ever since. 'The evening was a most successful one, and shows that the Scottish accountants in London have now thoroughly established themselves in the metropolis, and do not intend to allow their light to be hidden under a bushel'.

Whither the Profession? 1: Ahead of Enron

Anyone who thought that Enron and the outbreak of American corporate scandals in the early years of the 21st century was something new might be surprised to hear the views expressed about the quality of American auditing in 1897. In May of that year an Editorial in *The Accountants' Magazine* took issue with an article entitled 'English Audit of American Accounts' which had been published in another journal. This, we learn, had advanced the doctrine that 'true American railway accounting consists simply in expressing the situation as the board of directors see it'. *The Accountants' Magazine* was not going to let that stand. 'This view of an auditor's duty is not calculated to inspire the confidence of investors in American railways in this country', it thundered. 'If an auditor is merely to act as an expert revising bookkeeper to the board of directors, shareholders might not unnaturally ask wherein such an official served their interests. Even though it be admitted that the conditions affecting American railways are different from those prevailing in Great Britain, and that the rules which are applicable here would be inappropriate there, we cannot think that it would be impossible to obtain the services of auditors having the necessary special knowledge, who could safeguard the interest of shareholders without interfering unduly with the discretionary power of directors'.

Scots Outwith 4: Unique in Chile

In May 1904 an extremely bracing report on *Accountants in Chile* was received from the intrepid W J Kirkcaldie CA, writing from Iquique. 'Chile', he admits, 'will probably take rank as the *Ultima Thule* of an accountant reared in Scotland'. But he was enjoying his experience. And he was also, at that time, unique in Chile. 'I must apologise if I adopt an egotistical style, as our firm is the only one in the country, and consequently it is not possible for me to generalise'. Auditing the nitrate industry was their business and, while trains were a useful way of getting around, 'the service is not always convenient, and it is frequently necessary to ride from place to place. What would our brethren of the silk hat and the black coat say or think of the auditors arriving on horseback, booted and spurred as if on sport intent'. It was a very different life to that back home in Scotland. 'In one particular an auditor in Chile has to face a state of things which is not usually met with at home. Much of his work must be done in places where there are no hotels, and it becomes necessary to accept hospitality from those whose books are to be examined. Fortunately for us, the majority of people are disposed to be kind, but my own experience is that misunderstandings arise in quite unaccountable ways, and the personal and social element is a powerful factor in one's business duties'. And, of course, South America lived up to the old clichés. 'The laws in this republic are sound, but the administration is weak', he reports. 'Political questions are constantly cropping up, and one never knows where and how some revolutionary movement will start'.

Scots Outwith 5: Numbers

At the London dinner of the Association of Scottish Chartered Accountants in London in January 1903 Richard Brown of the Edinburgh Society told his audience that 'Scottish chartered accountants were increasingly proportionately at a higher rate than any other body of chartered accountants'. And he made the point that: 'Although so many of their members had emigrated to other countries and other parts of the United Kingdom, it was a fact that, so far as Scotland was concerned, they were better populated with accountants than any other part of the British Isles, for while in England there was only one chartered accountant to every 11,000 of the population, in Scotland there was one chartered accountant for every 7,000 of the population'.

Newfangled 3: Green Typing

Sir John Mann recalled his early experience with business machines in the 1870s.

I had been fascinated by a French Arithmometre calculating machine used in my father's office and an American Remington writing machine used by our family doctor. When I came into the office I experimented with both these curiosities, but found the calculator too clumsy for practical use and the products of the typewriter, (I bought it from the doctor for a trifle), too startling. Lawyers sent back typewritten letters "to be properly written". The press copies of the first of them, which I discovered years later in office letter books of October 1889, certainly look queer and un-businesslike, typed all in shaky capitals in green ink.

No wonder lawyers found them startling.

Scots Outwith 6: The Continent

Reporting from Paris in July 1904 Albert Finlay CA took a dim view of the French accountancy profession, divided as it was into innumerable different departments. After he has explained what, to him, is obviously an incredible state of disorganisation he then continues:

I may be pardoned if I introduce a personal reminiscence of my declaration au Prefet de Police. By law all foreigners intending to make a prolonged stay in Paris must declare themselves to the Prefet de Police within eight days of their arrival. I presented myself in fulfilment of this obligation, and on being asked my profession, replied: "Chartered Accountant". The official, with the usual French politeness, begged my pardon, as he did not comprehend my meaning. I repeated my reply and spelt the words for him. He answered that he had never heard the term, and asked me to explain the nature of the "trade". Naturally I protested against the word "trade", and claimed to be a member of a "profession". I informed him that he saw in me a liquidateur, a syndic, an arbiter-comptable, and a comptable expert all rolled into one. He refused to believe it, and said, "I shall put you down as a comptable", to which I replied that he could please himself, which he did. I mention this incident to emphasise that the chartered accountant is quite unknown to most Parisians.

The Fiftieth Anniversary

Landmarks in the progress of the various bodies which together make ICAS the oldest professional accountancy body in the world have been marked with dinners, speeches and peculiarities of their time. The first notable event was the fiftieth anniversary of the Society of Accountants in Edinburgh on 24 October 1904. A dinner was held at the North British Station Hotel and the great and the good duly pitched up. Sadly the Prime Minister was unable to be there. He was said to have 'expressed much interest in the Society, but was obliged to keep himself as free as possible from public engagements during the autumn recess'. Telegrams of good wishes arrived from fellow accounting bodies in New York, Illinois, Pennsylvania, California, Michigan, Missouri, Maryland, Bologna, Florence, Genoa, Naples, Milan, Marseilles, Brussels, Amsterdam, Stockholm, Peru, Uruguay and Havana, which gives us a good overview of the world of the Scots overseas.

In the style of the times the dinner ran to eleven courses, starting with oysters and taking in turbot, quail, lamb, raspberries and something called 'canapes Walter Scott'. The white wines were German, the Chateau Margaux 1890 and the Sandeman's Port 1890 must have been hugely enjoyable. They would have to be. The speeches were many and long. The third of the evening raised false hopes. 'I wish that I might stop here', announced Sir Ludovic J Grant, Bart., 'but that may not be. It is impossible for me to sit down without reminding you that the recent nocturnal vagaries of imperial forces other than our own have imparted a very special and a very solemn significance to the toast of the Imperial Forces of the British Crown'. Other speakers referred at length to 'the recent campaign in Thibet'. It was only after the fourth speech of the evening, and after Mr Robert Burnett had sung 'with fine effect' The March of the Cameron Men, that there was any mention of the reason for the evening. The Lord Advocate talked lengthily of the history of accountants before announcing that:

> *The result is that all of us who are favoured to meet them frequently, and happily or unhappily we lawyers have that fortune often, recognise them always to be men of capacity and skill, men of resource and suggestiveness, men of sterling integrity, men fitted to be what they are – honoured members of a learned profession.*

The President of the Society then gave a lengthy and exhaustive speech about how we got to where we are today. Amongst other attributes of the Society was 'a hall and well-stocked library, a strong and efficient company in the Queen's Rifle Volunteer Brigade (Royal Scots) and lastly, and what perhaps is considered the most important, a popular golf club'. Membership of the Society stood at 415 but a mere four out of the original 64 members from the foundation of the Society still survived. Lord Rosebery then spoke about Edinburgh and was followed by a response from the Lord Provost who, amongst many, many, other things said that he regretted to learn that Lord Rosebery disagreed with how Edinburgh spent its money. 'I regret to learn that from his Lordship because I was under the impression that Lord Rosebery was a citizen of Edinburgh'. At this point Rosebery made the key interjection of: 'Not a ratepayer!'. The Lord Provost then devoted much of his speech to lambasting Rosebery. Happily: 'Another song was given here by Mr Burnett'. Then George Touch, founder of the firm which would become, these days, Deloitte Touche Tohmatsu, spoke. He doubted whether the founders could have ever envisaged the growth in accounting that had occurred. That 'within little more than a generation from the time when those sixty-one gentlemen founded the first Society of Chartered Accountants, the Chartered Accountants in the United Kingdom would be numbered in their thousands, and that numberless societies of accountants would have sprung into existence in every quarter of the globe. The great English

Institute alone now has upwards of three thousand members, of whom only sixteen, I believe, and these the hardiest of them, have invaded Scotland. I hesitate to say how many Scottish Chartered Accountants have invaded England. The great majority of the English Chartered Accountants still remain in England, browsing on the fat pastures of England, which I have always regarded as the natural hunting-ground of the industrious Scot'. Another six speeches followed before the President brought events to a close.

Glasgow's Fiftieth

The 50th anniversary of the Institute of Accountants and Actuaries in Glasgow was celebrated on 15 March 1905. 'The Glasgow banquet', reported *The Accountants' Magazine*, 'although it had the disadvantage of coming after that of Edinburgh, and of being held at a less suitable season of the year, lacked nothing in enthusiasm, and considerably exceeded the Edinburgh meeting in numbers'. The Grosvenor Restaurant in Gordon Street was bulging at the seams. The opening speech declared of Glasgow:

> *You are the second city in the Empire, second to none in that spirit of corporate unity which places you even above the metropolis. Your argosies are in every harbour over the civilised world. The fleets built in your dockyards hold a proud position on every sea. The products of your markets pass into every land.*

The next speaker referred to 'the intolerable din of city life' and suggested better paving might help. When the evening eventually turned to accounting the President pointed out that there were now 454 members, including one present who was the only survivor of the original members. 'There are 56 of our members in England', he said, '46 in London alone, 16 in South Africa, 7 in India, 6 in the

United States, 3 in Australia, 3 in China, 2 in Central Africa, 3 in Central America, and others in Canada, Ceylon, Japan, Polynesia, Straits Settlements, and South America'. The next speaker said that 'the profession of accounting is pretty well scattered over the whole earth; and that if accounting be not co-extensive with civilisation, it is at all events co-extensive with commerce, which is pretty much the same thing'.

Sundries 2: Economy

In July 1907 members were informed of extracts from the diary of an Edinburgh Chartered Accountant covering 1827 to 1852, which *The Scotsman* newspaper, keen to boost its circulation, was then publishing. The diary was said to give 'an interesting picture of life in the Edinburgh of Sir Walter Scott'. The diarist turned out to 'have been present at the famous dinner when Scott disclosed his identity as the mysterious author of the Waverley Novels; and with true accounting instinct concludes a spirited account of the proceedings with the laconic sentence – "Ticket, £1, 1s"'.

Sundries 3: Taking care

Members were alerted in December 1910 to what was seen as a disgraceful new use of regulations. 'A number of business and professional men in Edinburgh', said the note, 'have received notices requesting them to pay inhabited house-duty on the full annual value of their offices, although, as a rule, only a very small portion of the premises is occupied by a care-taker as a dwelling-house. We are glad to notice that concerted action is being taken to resist this demand, which appears to be quite contrary to the law'. Poll-tax riots obviously had lofty forbears.

The First World War

The First World War, of 1914–1918, had a devastating effect. In November 1914 members were told that '*the war cloud which had so long hung over Europe has burst at last*'. The report continued:

> *To the accountancy profession as to the members of other peaceful occupations has come the opportunity of sacrifice and service. We publish this month a list of those, numbering over six hundred, who have left the offices of Scottish Chartered Accountants to join His Majesty's Forces. We wish them God-speed and a safe return. To those who are denied this privilege by age, ill-health, or the imperative call of other duties, we would offer as a consolation the reminder that he who helps to keep our financial and industrial machinery running smoothly and well is servicing his country as truly as he who risks his life upon the field.*

The magazine started to list deaths as well as those serving. 'Second Lieutenant James Bilsland, Scottish Rifles, killed, was also a member of the Glasgow Institute, having been admitted in 1913. He was recently recommended for the Military Cross and for promotion to a captaincy', being just one. By November 1916 under a heading 'The Cost of Unpreparedness', members were told of the problems with war expenditure and with the accounting. It referred to the Second Report by the Committee of Public Accounts for the year 1914–15. Talking of ship repairs it showed how in 1902–3 a system of net cost plus percentage system had been tried but had been found to be 'too costly'. Under wartime pressures:

> … in consequence of the extreme urgency of the work, there was no alternative but to adopt the net cost plus percentage system for almost all repairs, and for much of the new construction. The great objection to this system seems to be that the greater the amount spent on materials and wages, the greater is the contractors' profit. The Committee was informed that it was the duty of the local technical officers to report all cases of extravagance, and this was done from time to time, but action seems to have been taken in a few cases only.

Only one conclusion could be reached:

> It requires no Committee of Public Accounts to show that the condition of unpreparedness which existed in this country has enormously increased our war expenditure beyond what would otherwise have been necessary. But even granting that we were to do no more in peace time than we did do, towards the training of men and the provision of material, this Report makes it abundantly evident that if the problems which must inevitably arise on the outbreak of war had been carefully thought out beforehand, untold millions could have been saved. As things were the Government were at the mercy of contractors and manufacturers, and only too often had to pay for their lack of foresight to the uttermost farthing.

By June 1917 members were told that preparations were in hand for the eventual end of the hostilities.

> Perhaps the most difficult problem with which the profession will be faced after the war is the question of the re-instatement of the accountant students now serving in the army and navy. Apart from the small minority who are physically unfit, practically the whole body of apprentices have joined the forces. Many of these young fellows have now been under arms for nearly three years. On their return

to civil life their position will be one of peculiar difficulty. To men who have become accustomed to an open-air life the resumption of an existence in which their days must be spent in the confinement of an office and their nights in study will be unusually irksome. While they will probably retain most of the knowledge of accounts which they had acquired from their practical training, much of the book work will have been forgotten, habits of study will have been lost.

The conclusion was a wise one.

The men who return after the war will be very different from the boys who left their desks several years before. They will have learnt to take responsibility, to make decisions, to judge character – all faculties eminently useful to the professional accountant. These men are needed in the profession, and they may rest assured that they will receive every assistance and encouragement to take their places in it.

Meanwhile the casualties continued. In March 1918: 'Lieutenant-Colonel William Herbert Anderson CA, killed on 26th March … his three younger brothers having also fallen in the war'. He received a posthumous Victoria Cross. This was the citation, as printed in *The Accountants' Magazine*:

For most conspicuous bravery, determination, and gallant leading of his command. The enemy attacked on the right of the battalion frontage, and succeeded in penetrating the wood held by our men. Owing to successive lines of the enemy following on closely there was the gravest danger that the flank of the whole position could be turned. Grasping the seriousness of the situation, Colonel Anderson made his way across the open in full view of the enemy now holding the wood on the right, and after much effort succeeded in gathering the remainder of the two right companies. He personally led the counter-attack and drove the enemy from the wood, capturing twelve machine guns and seventy prisoners, and restoring the original line.

His conduct in leading the charge was quite fearless, and his most splendid example was the means of rallying and inspiring the men during a most critical hour. Later on the same day, in another position, the enemy had penetrated to within 300 yards of the village and were holding a timber yard in force. Colonel Anderson reorganised his men after they had been driven in and brought them forward to a position of readiness for a counter-attack. He led the attack in person, and throughout showed the utmost disregard for his own safety. The counter-attack drove the enemy from his position, but resulted in this very gallant officer losing his life. He died fighting within the enemy's lines, setting a magnificent example to all who were privileged to serve under him.

In January 1919 members were told that: 'The spectre of war, which has haunted us like a nightmare during these last four New Years, has, we hope, passed for ever from us'. And the Editorial in *The Accountants' Magazine* suggested that the world had returned to harsh financial realities. 'Included among our subscribers are a considerable number of apprentices', it said. 'We know there are many others who, although not on the list, buy the Magazine regularly. We would ask all such to become regular subscribers, and thus ensure the Magazine being delivered to them monthly. In every number of the Magazine there is something interesting to apprentices, and we are glad to have contributions from them, or inquiries about points on which they have difficulties'. The War was also a coming of age for the concept of income tax. In December 1918 'An Apprentice' wrote:

Several new departures have apparently taken place in most offices, which the apprentice in the army hears about only by remarks made by those carrying on at home, such as: "I must get on with the Income Tax work for Messrs Profitt, Mutch & Co". The apprentice also hears in a vague sort of way that the Income Tax work done for Messrs Profitt, Mutch & Co, is a very remunerative departure for the firm.

All in all some 391 members and 989 apprentices served in the War, this out of a total membership at the end of 1914 of 1,481. Sixty-eight were killed.

The Distaff Side 2: Tutorials

In June 1916 the Council of the Institute of Accountants and Actuaries in Glasgow opened all its tutorial classes 'to women who were serving as assistants in members' offices, and at the same time it was resolved to inaugurate a special elementary class to give women who had had some business training, but had only recently entered accountants' offices, a general training in simple bookkeeping and the elements of auditing and accounting practice'. It was discovered that this class 'met a felt need and proved very successful'. Indeed so successful was it that 'it was found necessary to divide the class into two portions'. Both were taught by Mr J J D Hourston who 'gives a very satisfactory account of the women students, and reports that they showed great interest in the work, and on the whole proved themselves thoroughly capable of mastering the elementary subjects embraced in his Prospectus'. 'It was only to be expected', concluded the report, 'that very few women would enrol themselves for the ordinary tutorial classes preparatory to the examinations, but in the one or two instances in which young women attended theses classes the tutors report very favourably on their progress. Until some definite arrangement is made for complete education and qualification of women in the accounting profession, it seems unlikely that many women will avail themselves of the more advanced classes'. By sheer coincidence the point is rubbed in by some news on the opposite page. At the AGM of the Institute of Chartered Accountants in England and Wales it was announced that a past-President, Mr Edwin Waterhouse, had resigned from Council. 'The vacancy thus caused', it was reported, 'was filled by the election of his son'.

Sir Ian Morrow:

Spanning The Modern Era

BY

Robert Bruce

Sir Ian Morrow, throughout his long career, has never shirked the task of telling people precisely what he thought of their management skills. Born in 1912 his career spans the whole of the modern era of business. When ICAS celebrated its Centenary in 1954 the man they called upon to close the event with a paper on '*The Place of the Accountant in Modern Society*' was Morrow. He pioneered the role of company doctor, sorting out enterprises as diverse as Kenwood and Rolls-Royce. He was President of what is now CIMA, the management accounting body, in 1956 and President of ICAS in 1981. He was still chairman of several companies that he was in the course of turning around when well into his eighties. At the last of the ICAS Summer Schools in 1996 he was giving as good as he got in the discussion groups. I can recall one lengthy conversation between him and a newly-qualified accountant from Glasgow on that occasion which was a model of venerable advice melding with the enthusiasm and zeal for change of youth. And even in his nineties in retirement in Saffron Walden in Essex he still lists 'ski-ing' amongst his recreations, though the intent is more mischievous than serious.

To gain a flavour of Morrow at his peak you perhaps should look at what he told the *Investors Chronicle* in January 1968. This was the era of an extraordinary price-cutting war in the white goods market. And, typified by the high profile failure of the time, John Bloom and the Rolls Razor enterprise, it all ended in tears. Morrow was brought in to save Kenwood from a disastrous venture selling cut-price fridges. Instead of cutting prices Morrow cut to the chase. 'I told him every time you get an order for a fridge, pin a five pound note on it and send it back, and you'll be better off', was his advice.

At the age of 94 he reiterates the same sharp advice when recalling his time at Rolls-Royce in the rescue days when he was made Deputy Chairman in 1971. 'Rolls-Royce was a classic case of very clever engineers thinking that management was something you learned at breakfast one day a week', he said. 'When I said they should close an order down they exploded and said that I didn't know what I was talking about and I would say "You will lose on that job"'. It was a simple tactic. Cash was more important than prestige. 'They were spoilt', he recalled, referring to the company's defence contracts. 'They just got lump sums from the Government'.

Sir Ian's insistence on clear thinking probably stems from his engineering heritage. His father was an engineer. In the Scottish tradition of the time he had worked in India. 'He was an enthusiastic engineer', said Morrow, 'and he was against me becoming an accountant but he said "It's your life". He taught me a hell of a lot. Why fuss about a few measly receipts when you should be fussing about the output of a £1 million machine'. And to give his son a flavour of what accounting would be about he found him a job not in an accountancy firm but in a jute mill in Dundee. 'They treated me like an engineer', said Morrow. 'I had to do the pay', he said, 'calculating the piece work. I was chased by the girls shouting "Hey laddie – you're two pence out"'. He smiles a mischievous smile. 'It was my first bit of accounting'. He qualified as an accountant in 1936. And then he left for industry. 'Scots accountants all went to London in those days', he said. 'I refused to go. I wanted to get out of the present profession and I wanted to start a new one'. He needed experience and he got it. 'I went to Macclesfield to a silk company which had been bought by a

US company which had put engineers in', he said. 'The accounting was all to hell. I worked twenty-four hours a day for six months and we got it right'. He had gained his experience and he had started to make his name.

'I wanted to set up a consulting firm', he said. This was heresy at the time. Accountants didn't do that. With his mentor at the time, Sir Lawrence Robson, the partnership of Robson Morrow was set up in 1942. 'Lawrence jumped at it', he said. But the ICAEW didn't. 'The English gave him hell', recalled Morrow. 'They were jealous of the fees we were getting'. The new firm found that the Morrow definition of consulting – "Please come and look at it, we are in a right mess" – provided a steady stream of clients willing to pay high fees to have their businesses saved.

It doesn't seem so revolutionary now. Consultants are ubiquitous. But it was different then. And Morrow still disapproves of how the current accounting firms go about it. 'I don't approve of taking people off audits and putting them into consulting', he said. The Robson Morrow model had different rules. 'People had to get a job for a year within an office or a business before we would have taken them on. Otherwise they wouldn't have known what we were talking about'.

His career as a company doctor burgeoned. His style is best explained through an article which the journalist Anthony Hilton wrote in 1970. This is how he described Morrow's position:

> *At the age of 58 Morrow has the kind of job most people dream about – an idyllic relationship with famous brokers. When in London he operates from an office in the heart of Hambros Bank. No money changes hands. Hambros pays him nothing, and even the furniture in his office is his own. But thanks to the Hambros link Morrow has emerged as one of the most gifted company doctors in the country.*

At the time Morrow summed up his philosophy simply: 'I believe in giving someone a job to do, backing him to the hilt, and leaving him alone to get on with it'. He still had the same fascination with engineering. At the height of the Rolls-Royce crisis he said: 'This is a quite awesome job. I am fascinated by the company and its technology. I love watching the wheels go round on the factory floor. And it's humbling to think there are only three companies in the world which can make this type of aero engine'. But having said that he continued: 'It takes a long time to get into deep water in the heavy engineering industry. But, once you're in, there is no easy way out'.

All this brought Morrow into close proximity to the wheels of Government as much as the wheels of heavy engineering. He still takes the view that politicians are not best placed to take decisions over business matters. 'I could go and see a minister', he recalled. 'They would say: "Tell us exactly what is happening"'. But the motivation was flawed. 'They didn't want to do something stupid and for people to say that the Government is an ass'. This was why, back in the early 1970s Morrow resigned after a run-in with Michael Heseltine, then an aviation minister. At the time he said of Whitehall generally: 'They are much more difficult than dealing with the banks because all the time they are bothered that they may make a big mistake and get blamed for it. And decisions are made for short term reasons so that a minister is popular, not so that it is good for the company or, indeed, the country'.

Morrow's views on the problems of the businesses he was brought into to sort out were clear. 'The primary causes of failure', he said, 'were not investigating an important investment properly, or bad management being appointed who didn't have the guts to fire the existing management. It has always been bad management. And the banks usually gave them too much money'.

His style was equally straightforward. 'I enjoyed going into a mess, being given complete power and control, otherwise I wouldn't go in. Telling them "I'm not going to fight you. I want it to work". And they would change, just like that. I didn't have to do much damage like firing people. It was more about sorting out what to do', he said. And then with another mischievous smile: 'A weekly meeting kept them sharp'.

His contribution to the Centenary conference back in 1954 is remarkable because so much of what he said has a resonance now. 'The basic concern of the profession has been', he said on that June afternoon fifty years ago, 'and must be, to perform the duties of public accountants, to serve the public with unquestioned integrity and to put the public need before personal needs, despite the impact of divided loyalties and conflicting interests, because the public accountant's aim is truth and justice as he sees it'. Those simple words echo down into all the post-Enron utterances of fifty years later.

It was a time when one of the greatest challenges came from the trend at the time for Whitehall to take control and try to run the nation's largest industries. Morrow's words are equally applicable to current arguments about measurement of the progress of health or education. 'In considering the place of the chartered accountant in industry', he said, 'it is perhaps desirable to make some distinction between nationalised industry and private industry. In nationalised industry a considerable amount of competition has been eliminated and management's concern is, firstly, to create in place of the yardstick of competition another means of measuring efficiency, and secondly, to overcome the problem of accountability, that is, in the case of public ownership, what is the check on management. Neither problem has been solved to anyone's satisfaction, but a great amount of work has been done, principally in the field of accounting by application of well-known techniques to provide a means of accountability, yet there is still a large field where accounting is of little help and where judgement alone can help'.

Equally Morrow talked of the future of the accountant in industry as one where they occupied the key strategic role. 'The accountant in industry today', he said, 'is expected to be a member of the management team along with the designers, the salesmen, the personnel officers and the production people. The accountant, because of his particular function, impinges on each and every one of the other functions'. This, said Morrow, was nothing less than: 'A revolution in thought, a revolution in attitude to what the accountant can and should provide in industry'.

He concluded his speech with two sections which foresaw much of today's accounting dilemmas. First he had this to say: 'Without an accountant's skills, modern society would not function. Today the practising accountant has gained the confidence of industry and commerce, both as an auditor and as an adviser. The problem is not that the industrial community will not turn to the practising accountant, but rather that they will expect from the practising accountant far more than he can reasonably accomplish. There is a danger that the span expected of the profession will exceed its grasp'.

And the second point, and his concluding words, were these: 'I have avoided as far as possible any predictions about the future, but if I may venture one suggestion it is that the profession may, in its next stage of development, have to decide whether it is going to follow law and medicine and consciously create specialists in the different fields, or whether it will continue to be satisfied with providing the basic training only'.

His views had not changed some thirty years later when he was interviewed for a special publication produced by *Accountancy Age* to celebrate its fifteenth anniversary in 1984. He lamented the profession's downgrading of what, to him, was a fundamental reason for its existence. 'They are trying to eliminate judgement', he said. They're trying to have great books of rules on everything'.

Those were the days when the mergers which ultimately created the 'Big Four' global accounting firms were just getting into their stride. He said that everyone in industry was asking: 'Where is the man that I can sit down and talk to about my accounting problems who will say, without going to a technical committee: "This seems to be a right balance"'.

His entrepreneurial enthusiasm was also undiminished. He thought that the largest firms would become unwieldy and unresponsive to their clients' needs and that forming smaller firms would be the answer. 'If I were a young guy today I would be out collecting four or five bright boys to set up', he said.

And in the end he produced the definitive reason why being a chartered accountant would remain a premier profession. 'Whatever happens', he pointed out, 'it seems that a chartered accountant always eats'.

His desire to continue working long beyond what many see as a reasonable retirement age was based, as all his decisions, on observation. Looking out over his garden in Saffron Walden he said: 'I watched people retire and in a year they were practically doddering old so-and-sos because they had nothing to look forward to'. Another ICAS president and friend of his, Jim McKinnon, retired from being head of OFGAS, the regulator for the gas industry, and took over a number of Morrow's non-executive roles. At the time he recalled Morrow's advice to him: 'When you retire always make sure you have your shoes on at breakfast'.

Sir Ian Morrow, at the age of 92, still has his shoes on at breakfast.

Robert Bruce was Editor of *Accountancy Age* from 1981 until 1990 and Accountancy Editor at *The Times* from 1992 until 2001.

Sundries 4: Health Tips

Keen members could glean some secrets of the success of the leaders of the profession in the obituary of Thomson McLintock published in March 1920. He played a good game of golf 'for one who first took up that pastime comparatively late in life' and he was fond of music and 'a regular attender of many of the concerts in Glasgow'. But the key was that: 'Mr McLintock kept himself fit by indulging in plenty of exercise and was a great walker. He invariably started the day by a walk of a mile or two before breakfast, and was very active right up to his death'.

Scots Outwith 7: No Publicity

In May 1924 the annual dinner of the Association of Scottish Chartered Accountants in London heard a fine example of what used to be referred to as the pawky sense of humour, and logic, of the Scots. The Association's chairman, Andrew Binnie, started by saying how sorry he was that the Secretary of the English Institute, owing to illness, could not be there. 'I am one of the many millions who listened to him when he recently broadcasted an address on "How to become a Chartered Accountant"', he opened:

If Mr Colville were here I would very much like to ask him how many of the millions had since applied to be articled, because I think we might possibly consider whether the scale of premiums for articled clerks should not be amended, not to meet the laws of supply and demand, which have long since gone out of fashion, but only to meet the increased cost of living. I feel bound to add that north of the Tweed, when we get hold of a good thing, we do not broadcast it; we keep very quiet about it and say nothing. I think that, if the secretary of a Scottish society were to broadcast at all, he would dwell on the serious disadvantages of the profession, the low fees, the hard work, the awful difficulty of construing the Income Tax Acts, which are absolutely obscure, and, above all, the great advantage of practising outside Scotland.

Scots Outwith 8: US Education

America was becoming the favoured far-flung destination of the CA. This passage, relayed to members from the American *Journal of Accountancy* for April 1907 shows why this was so.

While the young American accountant is today beginning his career with an education equal to that of the young English accountant, the same equality cannot be predicated when we compare Scotch and American requirements. A Scottish chartered accountant, in addition to examinations in all the subjects required in England, must also pass examinations in Actuarial Science and Political Economy. Scotland, therefore, must now be ranked as the pace-maker in the education of accountants. Let us hope that within ten years the educational standard in the United States will have risen from the English to the Scotch level, and perhaps have gone a few notches higher.

Scots Outwith 9: Fly Half

A member reported from St Paul, Minnesota in April 1912, that a local mystery had been solved. A missing $100 in the grain company accounts was the issue. 'Having gone over the books time and again, the accountant's pencil chanced to stop on an item of $150. The pencil point rested on the figure "one" when the figure suddenly broke in two and slid down the page. Upon examination it proved that the supposed figure "one" was a fly's leg which had become pasted in front of the 50'. More intrepid Scots sleuthing.

THE SCOTTISH CA ABROAD

BY

PETER JOHNSTON

An interesting indicator of the influence of ICAS members beyond Scotland is that, at the beginning of the 20th century, Scottish CAs constituted 25% of the entire British and Irish accountancy profession. Given the relative population of the regions within the British Isles and the large number of Scottish CAs that had already emigrated to countries around the world, this figure is impressive.

Notes of the Month in the February 1913 edition of *The Accountants' Magazine* reported on a meeting of the Glasgow CA Students' Society, when the subject was 'the Accountant Abroad'. It was reported that in the United States and Canada, the profession of an Accountant was of comparatively recent growth. The report went on to state that "the main features that distinguished work in America from work at home were the magnitude of the concerns dealt with and the great responsibility thrown on young Accountants. On the subject of salaries, Mr J A Gordon CA advised that those considering emigration "should not start in the United States for less than £300 (present day value, *ca.* £18,500) per annum". He went on to say that "Canada, and especially Eastern Canada, offered good prospects, Accountancy in the States at the moment being somewhat slack".

Interestingly, items in these notes also covered the Indian Companies Act, 1913, changes in the disciplinary scheme of the New Zealand Society of Accountants and an allocation of funds for staff salary increases then being proposed by "Mr. Ford, the owner of the well-known Motor Car Works in America". From this and other articles of the time, it is clear that there was keen professional interest in the wider world.

Students were warned at that 1913 students' meeting that "it would be better for an Accountant not to emigrate if his prospects at home were fairly good". Clearly, many Scots accountants and other professionals did take the plunge, since the January 1923 edition of that magazine carries a contributed article about the Scottish Gentlemen's Club of Canada, established in February 1922. By that time, it already had a membership of one hundred and was still growing. The main object of the Club was "to provide a 'hame frae hame' for (suitably educated) Scots abroad".

The early history of ICAS and the Scottish accountancy profession has already been well documented and this chapter focuses on the much more recent history. However, one further snippet from earlier times bears repetition, since it shows something of the enormous influence of the Scottish CA outside Scotland and gives a glimpse of the determination of the expatriate Scot to remove obstacles and get on with the job. The founder of what is now Deloitte Touche Tohmatsu in various manifestations around the world left Scotland to establish a branch office in London. He did so under his original Scottish surname Touch. That name is pronounced "Toogh". The "gh" particle has the Germanic quality found in the word "loch". The name proved very difficult for Londoners to pronounce. To make it easier for his clients and others, Mr Touch softened the pronunciation and the spelling to Touche and a new era dawned.

This little piece of history reflects a view that has been expressed so often by representatives of the profession around the world, namely that Scottish CAs are down to earth and hard working and that they settle in quickly and adapt well to a new environment.

This view was well stated by the then President of the Calcutta Club, who hosted the ICAS contingent during the 1994 visit by the ICAS President to members of the three British and Irish based

Institutes of Chartered Accountants, living and working in India. Giving a wonderful local perspective to his remarks, he said,

> *Of course, these Scotch CA fellows who came here were tip top and had the greatest possible reputation. They really rolled their sleeves up. Mind you, no accountants were allowed into this club until quite recently, you see. They were regarded as box-wallahs (merchants and businessmen) rather than professionals and so they were not eligible for membership, but that is all changed now.*

The Scottish CAs who left Scotland in the 19th century and early 20th century were essentially part of a much larger, pioneering migratory movement of that time. One Scottish CA, James Spencer Anderson, now deceased, who emigrated to Brazil in the late 1920's, spoke of business travel in a country where leprosy was still encountered. On business trips into the interior of the country, he was obliged to jump from the train before it reached the station, because lepers believed that they could be cured by biting any person who was not suffering from the disease. Spencer, as he was known to close friends, rose to great prominence in business in his country of choice, to the extent that he was granted audiences by the President of Brazil and was made a freeman of the city of Rio de Janeiro – a significant and unusual honour for a foreigner. His daughter remembers that he took his big American Buick car home on leave to Scotland and tells of him driving her up the west side of Loch Lomond on what was then little more than a single track road in "that bloody great car".

Anecdotal evidence and responses of CAs to questions posed at more recent receptions for ICAS members abroad suggest that many Scots who left for foreign climes after the Second World War did so for the experience or even "just for the fun of it". Many of those in practice were given this opportunity by the major accounting firms. Similar opportunities were given to CAs in business by the large enterprises they worked for. What is fascinating is that most went for eighteen months and are still there many years later.

One of the most pleasing aspects of the regular presidential visits to ICAS members around the world is that many of the members who attend these functions are nationals of the countries visited, rather than Scots. Typically, they came to Scotland and returned home after qualifying as CAs to work as accountants in their own countries. Many have achieved high office in government, industry and the profession in their own country.

In 1957, Sanford Yung Tao Yung CA, the first Chinese member in ICAS history, applied for a job with Lowe, Bingham and Matthews (later to become Price Waterhouse), Hong Kong. In his application, he stated that he wanted to work for this firm above all others, 'because it is Scottish' "and in accounting terms" he was later to attest, "so was I".

Unfortunately, pressure on training places and other difficulties have led to a proportionate decrease in numbers of foreign CA students and there is no sign of the flow being restored. Furthermore, as the accountancy profession develops in other countries around the world, the major accounting firms are now training home grown students in their own countries and regions.

In the larger centres, in countries where the greatest concentration of Scottish CAs and other expatriate accountants are found, clubs and other groups have been established and are generally flourishing. In countries with more scattered populations, these presidential visits often enable Scottish CAs to meet other CAs for the first time and to develop friendships. On more than one occasion, the President of the day has acted as an unwitting marriage broker to young CAs who have met up for the first time at an ICAS reception and subsequently tied the knot.

From the viewpoint of successive ICAS presidents and chief executives, these sometimes grand tours are as enjoyable as they are tiring. To outside observers, they can seem to be simply a holiday for those concerned, but they are usually linked in with other essential duties and functions and are always subject to time constraints. The travel involved is, to most, the least attractive feature. Typically, the trans-Canadian trek from Ontario to Vancouver, *via* Calgary and other major cities is undertaken in five days, following or followed by a conference or business meetings. Anyone who has worked their way across a country with three time zones in five days will understand how taxing this can be. Australasia presents similar challenges. The compensation is certainly to attend the receptions and to meet members, who are pleased that the President has taken the trouble to be with them.

It should be said that not all expatriate members are pleased with their Institute all the time. The question and answer sessions are not always relaxed. They do demonstrate that quite a few members abroad pay a great deal of attention to what is happening back in Edinburgh. They are not slow to offer advice, if they think that the President, Council or Chief Executive have got it wrong. Subscription levels can also be something of a hot topic.

Sometimes, things can go interestingly wrong – usually with travel, but sometimes with the actual arrangements. On one occasion, the bar staff managed to conceal a significant proportion of the stock during the reception and the organisers had to lock the doors at the end of the proceedings and help the bar staff to find the 'missing' bottles. On another occasion, the President and his retinue were sitting under a tree in a small airport, *en route* for the next location, when the announcement came from the loudspeaker tied to a branch of that tree, "Today's plane is coming tomorrow". In another continent, every pre-arranged flight (some eight flights were involved) disappeared from the airline computer at the end of the first day there and had to be recovered by the Chairman of the airline concerned.

From the standpoint of the Institute, the overwhelming feature of its overseas membership is its loyalty to the CA qualification and to ICAS. It is impossible for ICAS to offer any tangible services to its expatriate members. However, very few have actually resigned from ICAS membership for this reason. When asked why this is so, there are a few typical responses. One is that they worked hard for the CA qualification and do not want to lose it. Another reason given is that they have an attachment to ICAS and the old country and do not want to give this up. Some say that they do not even know how much they pay and do not see subscriptions as an issue. Whatever the reason, their ongoing membership is greatly valued, even if it is difficult for ICAS to express this in any material way.

It is interesting to observe changing patterns of emigration over the years. There are definite cycles, but it is difficult to attribute these clearly to any one factor, particularly since the reasons for these changes vary from country to country and from region to region.

This said, the most obvious reason for the downward trend of emigration by Scottish CAs during the last three decades of the 20th century has been the rapid development of accountancy professions and institutes in countries which previously relied mainly on imported skills. Changing structures and the development of local talent by the major accounting firms have also played an important part and the globalisation of finance, commerce and industry has contributed to the trend.

In the 1990s, much time and effort was devoted by accountancy bodies throughout the EU to agreeing the terms on which accountants from EU countries could be admitted to the profession in host countries of the EU. At the time, there was concern in various EU countries that large numbers of accountants would move in and cause problems to the profession in their country. In the event, very few chose to take advantage of the new freedom of movement. Those, including some Scottish CAs, who had already settled in other EU countries simply sat and passed the aptitude test and the related oral examination and thus obtained full practising rights in their country of choice.

As some doors have closed, others have opened. The need for rapid development or re-development of the accountancy profession in the countries of the former Soviet Union and elsewhere in Central and

Eastern Europe has led to a significant increase in outside accounting expertise. Along with other sister institutes, ICAS has been greatly involved in the export of its members' talents to assist these countries. Other Scottish CAs have taken the opportunity of moving to such countries with the major accounting firms, or as consultants.

Whatever direction future trends may take, history suggests that members of ICAS will continue to emigrate in numbers that are disproportionately high. In the past, economic pressures have led to mass emigration and these and similar pressures may yet play a part in encouraging ICAS members to move abroad.

The good news for ICAS is that the Scottish CA qualification has retained its value in the eyes of the outside world and that, in a rapidly changing world, people do still regard the Scots as born accountants, because they are seen as having the innate qualities of integrity, a sound work ethic and a sense of duty which underpins their formal professional skills.

The main point to be made in this context is that it has never been in any way necessary to be a Scot to become a member of ICAS and even if it is true that (some) Scots are born accountants, it is equally true that those of other nationalities assume these qualities as they pass through ICAS and emerge as Scottish CAs, if they did not already possess them.

Indeed, it is often rightly said that those who come in from the outside world are even more highly prized as ICAS members for having had the very good sense to do so!

Peter Johnston was Chief Executive of ICAS from 1989 to 1999 and Chief Executive of the International Federation of Accountants (IFAC) from 1999 until 2001.

Scots Outwith 10: Indignant Americans

By January 1915 the indigenous American accountants were starting to fight back against the invading Scots. 'A Scottish Chartered Accountant practising in the United States has sent us the following letter', it was reported, 'which was sent to one of his clients by a New York firm of Public Accountants.

Dear Sir,

This letter is simply written to remind you of our continued existence, and that, should you contemplate engaging accountants, we will be glad to call on you and tell you how and at what cost we do auditing, install modern accounting methods, &c. In short, we want to again bring our name before you'.

The letter concluded with a slogan. This read:

We were "MADE IN AMERICA". Use American Accountants, "NOT BLOOMING SCOTCHMEN".

As the Institute observed laconically:

It is satisfactory to learn that the Scottish Accountant seems to have made his presence felt in the States.

Sundries 5: Tax Appeals

In March 1925 members were informed of a report of an appeal before the Income Tax Commissioners against an assessment of £1,000 in respect of profits from carrying on the business of 'pitch and toss'. 'The assessment was upheld', and members were sternly warned that:

'This confirms the view that the profits of any calling, no matter how illegal it may be, are subject to assessment for the purposes of income tax'. The report also pointed out that: 'The appellant was described as a "tosser", and the description was not disputed by the appellant, who, however, disputed the amount of his profits'.

Newfangled 4: Trotters

Sir John Mann recalled early resistance to the new-fangled telephone. 'The telephone also had to overcome prejudice', he recalled in his reminiscences of 1954. 'It was at first erratic and troublesome. It had a mixed reception from the junior staff, the "trotters" as they were called; while they were relieved by the novel telephone conversations from being constantly sent out to deliver messages, verbal and written, they were deprived of the delights of the outings away from their desks and into touch with friends in other offices'.

Scots Outwith 11: Afloat

In August 1920 Sidney Mearns CA, describing himself as 'The Accountant Afloat', reported on life in the Navy as an Assistant Paymaster and in particular on the fancy financial footwork below decks. 'The arrival of a new Assistant Paymaster very frequently', he reported, 'coincided with a desire on the part of the Mess Secretary or the Wine Caterer to be relieved of the cares of office. Candour compels me to state that the average naval officer does not excel in the keeping of books of account, and the approach of the quarterly balance and audit is frequently attended by many heartaches and much head scratching'. He also recalled 'weary and nerve-racking days in a mine-sweeping sloop, of night patrols in mid-winter, and of uneaten breakfast in ships that would roll and cause grievous upheaval of the internal machinery'. Not surprisingly he concludes that: 'To a chartered accountant with the faintest spark of ambition it must be said, in conclusion, that the Navy can present but few attractions as a permanent vocation'.

Newfangled 5: Fear of Phones

Under the stern heading of 'The Telephone as a Business Intermediary' a warning was issued to members in February 1909 over the liability issues that this new-fangled business aid might exacerbate. 'Probably few of the inventions of modern science have proved of such practical use to commercial men as the telephone', said the reassuring preamble. 'In almost every office it is now recognised as an indispensable part of the business fittings'. But caution, as ever, was urged, in using it for business dealings. 'Just because it is so necessary and in such common use, it may be as well to remember that arrangements made by telephone ought to be confirmed by writing'. A recent court case presided over by Judge Rentoul, KC, in the City of London Court was used as an awful warning. 'The learned judge declined to hold that a man was necessarily bound by words passing over the telephone', it was reported. 'But in every case an arrangement made by telephone, qualifying a formal contract, ought certainly to be put afterwards into writing'.

Whither the Profession? 2: Royal Mail

The landmark court case involving auditors was The Royal Mail Case of 1931. This was in the days when 'true and correct' was the applicable audit opinion rather than the 'true and fair' rule which has been in place since 1948. The Royal Mail Steam Packet Company had been in trouble and to keep itself above water it had been transferring cash from undisclosed secret reserves to pay the dividend. The chairman and the lead auditor, one H J Morland from Price Waterhouse, were charged under the Larceny Act of deliberately misleading shareholders. Famously Morland's wife is supposed to have phoned the court on the day the verdict was expected to ask when he might be home for his tea. 'Probably in ten years time', the lawyer is said to have replied. Morland was cleared. The chairman went down for a year on another charge

It was a good result for the Scots. Sir William McLintock sorted out the mess and his firm won the audit. But it was a difficult issue to handle. 'There will possibly be some attempt to alter the law so as to strengthen the hands of the auditor and to give the shareholders more information about the Profit and Loss Account. That will not be easy to achieve', opined *The Accountants' Magazine*. It then wrestled with the problem. 'Would it not be a mistake to put, by legislation more directly upon the auditor, the responsibility of letting the shareholders know what the directors, in the interests of the company and the shareholders, decide to withhold? It should be remembered that secret reserves, in reason, are a sounder proposition than no reserves at all'. But in the end the opinion inched towards greater disclosure. 'There is no doubt that the situation as it has been left by this case presents great possibilities for the accounting profession', it suggested. 'It is not possible at the moment to forsee the probable repercussions of the case within the profession, but we are inclined to think that there will be a slight change of opinion towards meeting this alleged desire of shareholders to be told more, more especially in the Profit and Loss Account, or, if not shown there, in the auditor's certificate, or possibly verbally by the auditor at annual general meeting'.

Whither the Profession? 3: Revolting Peasants

At the Scots CA dinner in London in November 1970 the Director-General of what was then the Panel on Take-overs and Mergers, Ian Fraser, lambasted the accountancy profession. The report of the dinner said that:

> *Mr Fraser said that it was with the accountants that responsibility lay for the failure of communication which resulted when the public interpreted, in a different way from the accountants, financial statements compiled by the accountants. If the profession did not offer early results of its own from the work of its Accounting Standards Steering Committee, there might well be a "peasants' revolt". Politicians, stockbrokers, merchant bankers and financial journalists might try to impose an accountancy system of their own, which would be a pity.*

He then concluded that:

> *It was encouraging however to see how accountants were tackling the problem.*

Accounting Standards:
The Past 25 Years

by

Geoffrey Whittington

Accounting Standards in 1979

In 1979, accounting standards in UK and Ireland were set by the Accounting Standards Committee (ASC) which originated in 1970. Before 1970, there were no formal accounting standards in the UK. The impetus for setting up a standard-setting system came from Edinburgh – specifically from that remarkable controversialist Edward Stamp, the first full-time professor of Accounting at Edinburgh University (a Canadian CA who eventually became a Scottish CA). In the words of Sir Ronald Leach (1981):

> *In 1969 ... Professor Edward Stamp, then of Edinburgh University, came forth with a denunciation of the absence of firm accounting practices expressed with his customary vigour in a full-page article in The Times Business News. I was the unfortunate President of the English Institute at the time and was besieged by members demanding action from the Council to stem the mounting criticism of the profession in the Press.*

The English Institute's response was rapid: by December 1969 it had issued a Statement of Intent, and early in 1970, the new Accounting Standard Steering Committee (ASSC) was established as a partnership of the England and Welsh, Scottish and Irish Chartered Institutes. A leading Scottish proponent of the ASSC was Past President Sir William

Slimmings, one of the first members of the ASSC and subsequently (1976-8) Chairman of the ASC. In 1972, two more institutes, the Certified and Management Institutes joined the three partners and another institute, the public sector accountants' body CIPFA, joined in 1976.

By the end of 1979, the ASSC, now described by the briefer title, the Accounting Standards Committee (ASC) had published 15 accounting standards and 25 exposure drafts, a very creditable rate of output for a committee of part-time volunteers with limited staff support. The standards did not have the direct force of law, but they were widely followed and were therefore regarded as an important component of generally accepted accounting practice (GAAP). Thus, the ASC, at the end of 1979, could reasonably be regarded as a success.

However, with the apparent story of success, there were emerging difficulties which eventually (in 1990) led to the replacement of the ASC by the Accounting Standards Board (ASB). The most important of these difficulties was the ASC's lack of formal authority. It had been reconstituted in 1976 as a joint committee of the member bodies of the Consultative Committee of Accountancy Bodies (CCAB) and each standard, before issuance, was required to be approved by the Council of each of the six constituent professional bodies. When this approval had been won, it had only persuasive force: the approved standard would be evidence that the practices contained within it were generally accepted accounting practice, and therefore would be applicable to all accounts that were intended to give a true and fair view. However, this evidence was not necessarily conclusive and could, for example, be countered by evidence that alternative accounting treatments were widely accepted in practice. Thus, the ASC had to rely on persuading preparers of accounts and their auditors to accept its standards.

Related to this central difficulty was the fact that the ASC relied on the CCAB member bodies (particularly the ICAEW) for its staff and other resources. This not only meant that the resources were limited, but it also emphasised the dependence of the ASC on the professional bodies. Such dependence on one interest group became increasingly a disadvantage as the demand grew for the independent regulation of accounting standards.

These inherent problems were all apparent in the debate on inflation accounting which, by 1979, had reached a crucial stage.

The inflation accounting debate

Inflation accounting was the most difficult problem faced by the ASSC (and ASC) in the 1970s and it was to prove to be a critical element in the loss of authority of the ASC in the 1980s. By the time the ASSC was set up in 1970, inflation was already running at an exceptionally high level (in excess of 5 per cent per annum) by the standards of the post-war UK economy. In the 1970s this rose to double digit levels, peaking at more than 24 per cent in 1975, but still maintaining a double digit level in 1979. Conventional accounts did not reflect the impact of inflation, and there were calls for accounting standard setters to act.

The ASSC responded promptly by proposing in an exposure draft (ED8, 1973) that there should be supplementary inflation – adjusted financial statements. These would be adjusted on a general index (consumer price index) basis, which would not reflect the specific price changes of the assets and liabilities actually held by an entity. This was, in effect, a foreign currency translation exercise, translating historical cost in "old £'s" into a new currency, current £'s. This technical accountant's approach (known as CPP) did not appeal to the Government which appointed the Sandilands Committee to investigate the problem. This Committee was much less dominated by professional accountants than the ASSC (it was chaired by the non-accountant Chairman of a leading insurance company) and it recommended (at the end of 1975) an entirely different system, current cost accounting (CCA), which reflected changes in the prices of specific assets and liabilities, with no use of general indices.

In the following three years, the ASC, and particularly its Inflation Accounting Steering Group (led by the Edinburgh-educated former ICAEW President, Douglas Morpeth) fought doughtily to resolve the conflict between CPP (advocated earlier by the ASSC and still supported within the auditing profession) and CCA (advocated by Sandilands and the Government, and with some support from industry). An early attempt to introduce CCA (ED18, 1976) was withdrawn after a revolt by members of the ICAEW, led by small practitioners (the Keymer and Haslam resolution). Voluntary interim guidelines were then introduced (the Hyde Guidelines, 1977) and finally a draft standard (ED24) was published in 1979. This attempted to reconcile CCA with CPP by introducing gearing and monetary working capital adjusted into what was basically a CCA system. It also required only supplementary statements rather than (as in the case of Sandilands and ED18) the price-change adjustment of the main accounts, and it applied only to large companies.

Thus, in 1979, the ASC was on the verge of making a critical decision, in an attempt to resolve a problem that was not of its own making (the inflation rate and the Government's intervention being critical factors). In 1980 it took the crucial (and, with hindsight, fatal) step of issuing SSAP 16, a current cost accounting (CCA) standard embodying the compromise features of ED24. At first, almost all of the companies to which it applied followed SSAP 16, but events in the wide economy soon had an adverse effect. A new government, led by Margaret Thatcher, had been elected in 1979, and it was committed to a tight monetary policy. In 1982, the annual rate of inflation declined to 5.4 percent, and it continued to fall (by 1986 it was 3.7 per cent). At the same time, the policy of the new government was to dismantle price and income controls, in the context of which CCA accounting was attractive to many firms (since it tended to raise reported costs and lower profits). Moreover, in 1982, a Green Paper on Corporation Tax recommended that CCA adjustments should not (as some had hoped) become allowable as tax deductions. Thus, there was a falling off in support for CCA, and this support had never been overwhelmingly strong.

The result was a sharp decline in compliance with SSAP 16, which posed a serious threat to the ASC's authority. Attempts were made to find a more acceptable compromise, but it was clear that there was no solution to the CCA/CPP controversy that would command support. As an alternative, the ASC sought to establish its authority at law, by taking Counsel's opinion. The result was the well-known Hoffman–Arden opinion (1983) which asserted that the ASC's standards were authoritative guidance in determining the generally accepted accounting practice that would give rise to a "true and fair" view. However, by 1984, only a minority of the relevant companies was producing supplementary CCA information under SSAP 16, so that, in practice, the standard could not be said to be "generally accepted".

The ASC made a further brave attempt at compromise (ED35, 1984), but in June 1985, the mandatory status of SSAP 16 was withdrawn, thus recognising the reality that it was widely ignored. The standard was not finally withdrawn until 1988 because one CCAB body (the CACA) refused to endorse withdrawal until then. Both the collapse of SSAP 16 and the ASC's inability independently to withdraw it illustrate the weakness of the ASC's position, which had been cruelly exposed by the inflation accounting controversy.

The problem of creative accounting

At the same time as the ASC's authority was being challenged in the inflation accounting controversy, a new challenge was arising in the form of creative accounting. This is not a single technique but a range of techniques intended to manage profits, gearing ratios or any other accounting measures that were important to investors and lenders. The object was to gain an advantage in increasingly competitive capital markets, in which financial engineering was becoming a science (or possibly an art form) as liberalised markets extended, deepened, and provided a new and complex range of financial products. Unsurprisingly, these methods tended to be applied particularly when firms were going to the market for new funds, as in a takeover situation. In this sense, the wheel of history had turned full circle: it was problems associated with large takeovers (notably GEC-AEI and Leasco-Pergamon) that had provoked the calls for the ASSC to be established in 1969.

The techniques of creative accounting were described persuasively in 1986 in a book by the accountant journalist Ian Griffiths, entitled *Creative Accounting*. The sub-title was even more explicit: "how to make your profits what you want them to be". In it were described an impressive range of techniques, including off-balance sheet financing, reorganisation provisions, goodwill write-offs to equity and many others, with illustrations from actual cases. Even more striking in the latter respect was the later book, *Accounting For Growth*, by the city analyst, Terry Smith (1992) which "named names", listing the creative accounting practices of many leading companies, illustrated by extracts from their accounts and supported in some cases by quantitative estimates of the effect on the accounts of these practices. This book cost Terry Smith his job, but this event increased public curiosity and the book ran to a second edition (1996). It does not appear to have affected his career as he is currently Chief Executive of the brokerage firm Collins Stewart.

The ASC was, of course, aware of these developments and, bearing in mind the limits of its powers and resources and the demands of the debate on SSAP 16, it was very active in producing standards in the 1980s. By the time it finished its work in July 1990, the ASC had issued 25 original standards (10 of them since 1979), nine of which had been revised and reissued and three had been withdrawn. It also left behind ten exposure drafts that had not become standards. These included ones that dealt with some difficult and controversial topics which might have created further challenges to the ASC's authority. Notably, ED 47 dealt with *Accounting for Goodwill* (on which there was already a standard, SSAP 22, which had been revised once and, in its current form, encouraged the immediate write-off of purchased goodwill) and ED 49 *Reflecting the Substance of Transactions in Assets and Liabilities* (containing the "substance over form" approach to dealing with creative, particularly off balance sheet, accounting). Another potentially controversial exposure draft was ED 53, on *Accounting for Acquisitions and Mergers*, which proposed to tighten up the qualification criterion for merger accounting (pooling of interests) in the existing SSAP 3, which had been the subject of considerable abuse, through such devices as vendor placings (nominally making an acquisition by share issue, but providing an attractive guaranteed cash alternative).

However, the ASC was spared the problems of implementing these exposure drafts as standards because, at the end of July 1990, it was dissolved and replaced by the new Accounting Standards Board, as a result of the implementation of the Dearing Report.

The Dearing Report and the new ASB structure

The collapse of support for SSAP 16 and the emerging problems of creative accounting led the CCAB, in the autumn of 1987, to initiate a fundamental review of the standard-setting process. The Committee was chaired by Sir Ron Dearing (later Lord Dearing), a former senior civil servant and Chairman of the Post Office Corporation. The report, *The Making of Accounting Standards*, was published in September 1988. Most of its recommendations were implemented in the Companies Act 1989, insofar as they required legal backing, and the new institutional arrangements were put in place in 1990.

The essence of the Dearing proposals was to maintain accounting standard-setting as a private sector activity, but to widen its base and make it independent of the direct influence of professional bodies. The new organisation would be much better funded and resourced than the ASC, and its standards would have greater authority derived from the Companies Act. The latter proposal (legal authority) was not implemented in as strong a form as the Dearing Report suggested, but otherwise the new ASB/FRC system conformed substantially to the Dearing template.

As the head of the new standard-setting institutions was the Financial Reporting Council (FRC) whose Chairman was appointed jointly by the Secretary of State for Trade and Industry and the Governor of the Bank of England. The membership of the FRC was widely representative of industry, the accounting profession and other interested parties, such as fund managers and trade unions. Its role was to raise funds (which included a government contribution, as well as private sector donations) appoint members of the Accounting Standards Board (ASB) and Financial Reporting Review Panel (FRRP), and monitor the work of these bodies, without intervening in their day-to-day functions. The ASB had a full-time Chairman and Technical Director, who were voting members of the Board, plus (initially) seven part-time members. All Board members were paid for their work, and provision was made for a full-time technical support staff. The standards were to be issued on the ASB's own authority, without formal approval from any other body. Under the 1989 Companies Act, accounting standards were defined and preparers of accounts were required to describe their compliance with the standards and to explain departures from them. If accounts failed to comply with the requirements of the Act a court could order the preparation of revised accounts, at the directors' expense: an ingenious and effective penalty. The "missing link" in the legal authority was that the Act did not explicitly require that accounting standards should be followed (as

Dearing had recommended), although there was a strong incentive to do this, given that departures had to be justified. Compliance was assisted by the FRRP, another committee of the FRC, chaired by an eminent lawyer, which could, in response to complaints, initiate court proceedings to remedy non-compliance with the accounting provisions of the Act.

The ASB, 1990–2000

The first chairman of the ASB was David Tweedie, a Glasgow-trained CA, who presided over the first decade (1990 – 2000). The first Technical Director was Allan Cook, who held office for even longer (1990 to 2003) and together they formed a powerful team. During the first decade, the ASB issued 19 new standards (FRSs) plus the Financial Reporting Standard for Smaller Entities (the FRSSE) and a Statement of Principles for Financial Reporting (the conceptual framework that underpinned the ASB's work). Additionally, the ASB franked a number of SORPs (Statement of Recommended Practice) issued by approved industry committees, and its Urgent Issues Task Force (UITF) issued 27 Abstracts. Outside the formal standard-setting process, the ASB contributed to the international convergence and development of accounting standards, particularly through its membership of the "G4+1" group of standard setters, which was increasingly active during the period. A direct link with international standard-setting was created when David Tweedie became one of the UK members of the IASC in 1995.

A number of the ASB's standards issued during this period were innovative and have had (or are still having) a significant impact internationally. Notable examples are FRS 3, FRS 5, FRS 10 and FRS 17.

FRS 3 (1992) *Reporting Financial Performance* re-cast the income statement. It clarified the separate effect of acquisitions and disposals and it (effectively) abolished the concept of extraordinary items, which had been the subject of much abuse. It provided a framework for reporting performance which was more transparent than previous practice, and it introduced a new primary statement, the Statement of Total Recognised Gains and Losses (STRGL), which added to profit and other gains and losses recognised in the year to produce a total which would now be called comprehensive income. The rest of the world still has to catch up with this innovation: the US (FASB) has a statement of comprehensive income but it is not a primary statement and lacks the prominence and clarity of the STRGL. The IASB (in IAS 1) has a Statement of Changes in Equity, but this does not (except in an optional format) make a clear separation between comprehensive income and other sources of changes in equity (such as capital contributions by owners). The ASB produced a further proposal (FRED 22, 2000) to revise FRS 3 by producing a single performance statement, combining the profit and loss account with the STRGL, but this was deferred as a result of the need to work with the IASB towards a converged international solution, or, as some might say, to allow the rest of the world time to catch up.

FRS 5, *Reporting the Substance of Transactions* (1994), was aimed directly at creative accounting practices. It had its origins in ED 42 and ED 49, issued by the ASC (and in a 1985 technical release, TR 603, issued by the Institute of Chartered Accountants in England and Wales). It adopted a substance over form approach, requiring firms to base their reporting on the true commercial effect of transactions. It developed the concept of a "*quasi*-subsidiary" to deal with entities (such as some securitisation vehicles) that were not legally subsidiaries but were so in economic effect. The standard was not universally popular and was particularly opposed by those involved in the complex financial engineering processes underlying off-balance sheet financing, but it was, in due course, accepted and later, when the Enron collapse and other accounting-led scandals arose in the US, the British financial community was grateful to have FRS 5 in place.

FRS 10 *Goodwill and Intangible Assets* (1997) dealt with another area which had been a focus of creative accounting and had already been visited twice by the predecessor body, the ASC. The FRS 10 solution was arrived at after public hearings (a unique event, to date, in the ASB's history) and was controversial, but it has achieved acceptance in the UK and has had a clear influence on standards adopted later by the FASB and the IASB. The central proposal of FRS 10 was that goodwill should be capitalised and amortised over a period not exceeding 20 years when it had a finite life. It was also to be subject to an impairment test (contained in the companion standard, FRS 11) on initial acquisition and whenever there was an indication of impairment. Where it could be demonstrated that acquired goodwill had an indefinite life, it need not be amortised but was subject to an annual impairment test. The treatment of purchased goodwill matched that of other intangible assets, so that there was no longer any incentive for accounting arbitrage between recognising intangible assets and goodwill in a business acquisition. The impairment testing approach to accounting for purchased goodwill was taken a stage further by the later US standard (FAS 141), which banned amortisation and required annual impairment testing. This approach was subsequently adopted by the IASB (IFRS 3, 2004).

FRS 17, *Retirement Benefits*, was published in December 2000, in the last month of Sir David Tweedie's chairmanship of the ASB. It made controversial proposals with respect to defined benefit pension obligations. These were now to be recorded in the employing company's balance sheet at their current value (present value of the discounted expected cash flows for the liability, less market value of investments backing the obligation). Changes in that value were to be recorded in two ways: current service costs were to be charged to the profit and loss account (where interest on the liability was to be charged and investment returns credited), but the actuarial gains and losses, resulting from changes in estimates of existing obligations and changes in the value of the investment, would be recorded in the STRGL. Although this recognised the important distinction between the current costs of the pension scheme and the large changes in value arising from changes in expectations (including changes in the market value of investments), the idea of recording the total impact of these changes in the accounts as soon as they occurred was shocking to many preparers of accounts. The existing standard (SSAP 24) inherited from the ASC, adopted an actuarially smoothed method of recording pension costs in the accounts. The current US standard (FAS 87) and the international standard (IAS 19) also allow an option to smooth recognition (which is widely adopted in practice) although their basic method of calculating the pension obligation (as required to be revealed in supplementary disclosures to the accounts) is similar to that of FRS 17. Thus, FRS 17 was a world-leading standard, but that was not a comfortable position to be in when large actuarial losses were in prospect, due to the decline of stock market (reducing investment value) and the increase in the expectation of life (increasing the liabilities). Sir David's successor, Mary Keegan, inherited the thankless task of persuading the UK preparer community that FRS 17 incorporated the appropriate direction for the future of pension cost accounting.

Thus, in its first decade, the ASB managed to use its new powers and resources to considerable effect. There was controversy about particular standards, and about the statement of principles, against which Ernst & Young, led by Ron Paterson, the Scots accountant heading up their technical department, mounted a campaign, but the ASB suffered no setbacks comparable with the ASC's problem over non-compliance with SSAP 16. There also continued to be occasional "accounting scandals", but the most prominent of these (such as the collapse of BCCI and of the Maxwell companies) were associated with non-compliance with standards and fraud, rather than with the failure of the standards themselves. This is not to say that creative accounting had disappeared, but it was on the retreat. Equally, the standard-setting body was not on the retreat. The ASB's acceptance as part of the established system of regulation was demonstrated by the award of a knighthood for its chairman, David Tweedie and a CBE to its Technical Director, Allan Cook. These were the two full-time board members during the first decade, when the ASB established itself.

The influence of International Accounting Standards, 2001–4

The next change in the standard-setting scene came quite abruptly in 2000, as a result of the Lisbon Agreement between the finance ministers of the European Union (EU) member states. This stated that all companies listed on EU stock exchanges would be required to prepare their consolidated accounts on the basis of International Accounting Standards, as approved by the EU, with effect from 1 January 2005. This decision was not only sudden, but the timetable was very demanding, in view of the fact that the IASC had only just completed its standards for endorsement by IOSCO (the international organisation of securities regulators) and IOSCO had made a large number of suggestions for improvements, which would entail significant work before the standards were finalised.

The IASC was replaced by a new body, the IASB, to cope with these new responsibilities. Our concern here is not to follow the work of the IASB (a story in its own right) but to record its impact on the ASB. Clearly, listed UK companies (or at least the vast majority that produced consolidated accounts) would, in the near future, be complying with international standards. For the ASB, this raised the issue of convergence with international standards: clearly, it was undesirable to have two distinct accounting languages in the UK if this could be avoided. In the short term, the ASB was confronted with another problem, in that its Chairman, Sir David Tweedie, left at the end of 2000 to become Chairman of the new IASB.

The latter problem was resolved by the appointment of Mary Keegan as Chairman of the ASB. Formerly, she had been director of global reporting at PricewaterhouseCoopers, which gave her an ideal background for managing the process of co-ordination and convergence with the IASB.

The ASB's work with the IASB since 2001 has followed two distinct paths. First, the ASB has developed a programme of converging its standards with those of the IASB and has issued a number of exposure drafts designed to enable this. In some cases, the convergence is likely to be complete, whereas in others the ASB is likely to converge as much as is practicable and desirable, given that IASB standards are in a state of change and the ASB has established standards that are currently working well and might be regarded by some as being ahead of current international standards (*eg* FRS 3 and FRS 17, which were discussed earlier).

Second, the ASB is working with the IASB as one of the eight standard-setters that have a designated liaison relationship. This involves developing joint projects. Currently active ASB/IASB projects include those on Reporting Comprehensive Income (which now also involves the FASB) on Leasing (currently in the research phase) and on Service Concessions (intended to lead to an IFRIC interpretation). It also involves monitoring the IASB's work more broadly, through technical comment at all stages of projects and through exposure of IASB drafts to the ASB's constituency. As a result of this relationship, the ASB has been able to give authoritative public support to the IASB on such important issues as the new standard on accounting for share based payments (IFRS 2).

Apart from its work with the IASB, the ASB still has a distinct domestic role as the standard-setter for those companies in the UK and Ireland that are not listed and for listed groups until 2005. One of the more difficult problems has been the status of FRS 17, the adoption of which was made optional, pending the adoption of international standards by listed companies in 2005. The IASB is trying to introduce an option into IAS 19 which will enable, in effect, the adoption of FRS 17 accounting within IAS 19. This will mean that UK companies that adopted FRS 17 will not be forced back into a smoothing regime when they adopt international standards. Within the UK, although FRS 17 was made optional, Mary Keegan fought a doughty battle to persuade UK preparers of the merits of the new standard, and acceptance of it is becoming more widespread. Increasingly, preparers of accounts are recognising that the underlying costs of funding defined benefit schemes are made more transparent by FRS 17.

The ASB also has a range of other activities, notably through its public sector committee, which applies the standards to public sector activities (which are outside the IASB's scope) and the UITF, which gives prompt interpretations on urgent issues not explicitly dealt with by existing standards. The Review Panel has recently assumed a more pro-active role in seeking out non-compliance with accounting standards and seems likely to play a vital role in enforcing compliance with both ASB and IASB standards in the future. The ASB has also been given responsibility for prescribing the contents of the enhanced Operating and Financial Review, recommended by the recent Company Law Review. The ASB was also asked by the Secretary of State for Trade and Industry in March 2004, to make recommendations for improving accounting for with profits life assurance contracts. This request resulted from the Penrose Report on the problems of Equitable Life Assurance Society. It relates to an area with which international standards are unlikely to deal adequately for several years (an international project on insurance has already run for several years, and the industry internationally has no shared vision of the appropriate solution). It provides a good example of how national standard setters, such as the ASB, still have a role in a world where international standards are accepted.

In summary, despite the creation of the IASB and the adoption of its standards for use by listed companies, the ASB has many roles to play. If anything the ASB has more, rather than less, to do as a result of the advent of the IASB. The challenge for Mary Keegan's successor (after she left to become Managing Director, Financial Reporting and Audit at HM Treasury, in July 2004) will be to focus these activities in a coherent manner which ensures that the ASB continues to be a distinct voice in world standard setting.

Geoffrey Whittington is the member of the International Accounting Standards Board with responsibility for liaison with the UK standard-setting body, the ASB. He is Emeritus Professor of Financial Accounting at Cambridge University and a member of the ICAS Research Committee. From 1972-75 he was Professor of Accountancy and Finance at Edinburgh University, where he introduced honours degrees in accounting for the first time, and from 1996 to 2001 he was Professorial Research Fellow of ICAS.

The Distaff Side 3: Surplus Fees

It was reported that on 9 October 1916 at the Hall of the Society of Accountants at 27 Queen Street in Edinburgh Mr J Stuart Gowans CA, 'delivered the opening lecture of a series which he will give weekly on Monday afternoons at 5.30 to women assistants employed in accountants' offices'. The subjects included 'Book-keeping, Auditing, (Commercial and Trusts), Bankruptcy, Liquidations &c'. It was reported that 'the large enrolment of sixty-five is evidence of the great interest taken by women assistants in the means provided to increase their usefulness'. Further: 'The fee payable by each student for the course is 10s., but Mr Gowans is generously giving his services gratuitously. At the close of the lectures it will be decided to what good object the fees will be applied'.

Scots Outwith 12: Chinese Bandits

In April 1924 advice on whether CAs should hotfoot it to work in China came from a CA resident in Shanghai. He started with the cheering news that 'wines and cigars are cheaper than in London, and better too' but concluded that 'on the whole, living is more expensive in Shanghai than in London, but living out there embraces many small items which in London would be considered luxuries'. The prospects were good but the politics unsteady. 'There is plenty of work and scope for young CAs in China', he reported, 'and one would always be welcomed by his professional brethren in Shanghai. Trade in China is at present very much handicapped by the political situation in the interior of the country; the absence of a central control over provincial armies and ex-armies, (ie, soldiers who, not having been paid for two or three months, change their profession and become bandits), naturally has a most depressing influence on all trade. Such, however, cannot be a permanent condition, and meantime the supply of young CAs is not in danger of exceeding the demand'.

The Distaff Side 4: A Society

In November 1916 it was reported that:

In reply to a question by a member, the President stated that the admission of women to the profession had been considered by the Councils of the Edinburgh Society and the Glasgow Institute and by the Joint Committee. The Edinburgh Society and the Glasgow Institute had been advised that under their charters they had no power to admit women. The Joint Committee had considered the question of the training of women at a recent meeting, and had expressed their readiness to consider any reasonable scheme that might be submitted to them; and it was understood that two members of the profession, one in Edinburgh and one in Glasgow, who were particularly interested in the question, were to prepare such a scheme and submit it for the consideration of the Committee. It was hoped that along these lines the way might eventually be opened for the formation of a Women's Society of Accountants in Scotland.

The Distaff Side 5: Comfortable

In December 1919 the implications of the passing of the Sex Disqualification (Removal) Bill by Parliament were discussed.

A great extension of the activities of women will thus be made possible, and a problem which has for some time been engaging the attention of the governing bodies of most professional societies will be taken out of their hands and solved at one stroke. In the accountant profession, as in others, any legal obstacle to the admission of women to the various societies will be removed.

It was reported that on 30 October at the quarterly meeting of the Glasgow Institute a resolution 'to take steps to have the Constitution altered or amended so as to permit of women being admitted as members' had failed to command the required majority. 'Be that as it may' said the report, 'it can be assumed that even the most resolute opponents of the reform will accept the inevitable with good grace, and that women will now find no difficulties in the way of their admission to the societies, apart from the passing of the examinations and the fulfilment of the other necessary conditions of membership'.

It transpired that the opposition in Glasgow came 'mainly from the younger members'. 'The majority of these have been serving in the army for years, and some of them no doubt feel that the difficulties in the way of resuming their civil vocation are already serious enough without the addition of competition by a flood of women accountants. This may not be the ideal attitude', said the report, 'but it is a not unnatural one. We are inclined to think, however, that the prospect of such competition has been much exaggerated. Women have not so far exhibited any overpowering desire to become Chartered Accountants. Happily for the nation, most girls look forward to marriage as their ultimate destiny, and therefore regard any occupation they may have taken up as a stop-gap. It may be doubted whether many, even of those who have done such good service in accountants' offices during the war, will care to undertake a long, arduous, and expensive training, which will be of little use to them if, in the end, they adopt the ancient and honourable profession of looking after a house, husband, and babies'.

Newfangled 6: Automation

In November 1936 one Ralph Curtis administered some wise words to members on 'The Accountant and the Machine'. Automation was taking its toll. 'The very great strides which have taken place in the technique of office organisation during the past ten years', he suggested, 'have laid a heavy burden of responsibility on to the shoulders of the accountancy profession in several directions'. As ever audit problems loomed. 'In how far can he accept the machine figures as correct?', for example. And cost-cutting was also a possibility. 'How far is the posting from one book to another completely automatic, and in consequence how much of his detailed check can be dispensed with?' And what about fraud? 'What are the possibilities of human error, still more what are the possibilities of protection against fraud?' And what of the problems created when the audit client has not consulted with his accounting firm before making the crucial decision of what machine to buy. 'Most accountants', says the advice, 'are familiar with the disgruntled businessman who has installed a machine-accounting system and has been very disappointed and very dissatisfied with the results. In every case such dissatisfaction can be traced to the fact that the customer has yielded to the blandishments of some particularly silver-tongued machine salesman'. Systems like this would also lead to dilemmas for the auditor. 'If the auditor can obtain from a reasonable number of the customers and suppliers of the concern written agreement as to the balances on their accounts, I would suggest that even the check from the original documents to the prime books is unnecessary'. The author could hear the hiss of the word heresy at this suggestion. 'I am aware', he writes, 'that such an idea will be regarded in some quarters as being completely revolutionary, but I am convinced that much time is taken up in checking original documents which mean nothing at all'. He is also very impressed at machines which sort punched cards. 'It is not, however necessary', he points out, 'to search the cards for circular holes, as a machine has been invented into which all cards thus punched can be placed, and which will run through the cards at an almost incredulous speed, and will throw in automatically a red card alongside every card bearing a circular hole'. As a result the auditor will be freed from his old routine and 'he will then be able to devote his whole attention to the loopholes which still exist for error or fraud – matters with which no machine system can deal'.

Sundries 6: Advisory

The advice given by the President of the Edinburgh Society to newly-qualified members in July 1939 contained this passage:

As I have said before, do not be discouraged if, in this testing period, the remuneration which is offered to you is, in your estimation, much less than it ought to be. It may be news to you, but it is true, that those who think more about their work than their wage reap higher ultimate rewards than those who think more about their wage than their work. This remark applies to fees as well as to salary, as you will find, when you reach the happy stage of rendering fees to clients.

You can almost hear the shuffling of feet amongst the audience.

Scots Outwith 13: Favouritism

The dogged pioneering ways of the CA abroad was most definitely required in America as is made clear in this note on the professional life of CAs in America which members received in August 1924. 'It must be remembered that the accountant who comes to America today will find conditions very different from those encountered by the pioneer accountant of thirty years ago', it started. 'The young American practitioner is today almost invariably a graduate of a college located in or near one of our large cities, and most naturally starts practising in the same city where he has his circle of friends. The foreign accountant should therefore be prepared to go to the more undeveloped sections where the need for accountants, though not immediately great, will nevertheless develop. There he will not meet the favouritism resulting from college friendships, and will receive the slow but sure reward of the pioneer'.

Scots Outwith 14: School Ties

In May 1924 a short note appeared on the life of the CA in the Philippine Islands, 'where', as the author helpfully pointed out, 'the hemp comes from'. 'Social life means something in all cities of the Far East', he remarked, 'and that is probably why one notices in the advertisement columns so many demands for public school men. Everyone cannot, of course, be of Fettes or Loretto. Still it helps'.

Scots Outwith 15: Camaraderie

The networking and camaraderie of the Scots CAs running the Empire in the inter-war years comes through strongly in the Institute archives. In May 1925 one CA sent back an account of life in Japan. He concluded with this evocative ending: 'At Penang I was introduced to another Edinburgh CA, so any one travelling east can look forward to meeting fellow-accountants at most of the ports on the way'.

Scots Outwith 16: Go Forth

It was small wonder that so many CAs went off to the Empire between the wars. Members were told in January 1931 that: 'For the young man who is prepared to go abroad the starting salaries are higher, and there is a sure prospect of success; the appointments are many'.

The Second World War

Quoting the lines:

> *if ye break faith with us who die / we shall not sleep, though poppies grow / in Flanders fields*

the editorial of *The Accountants' Magazine* of November 1939 announced that: 'It is humiliating to read these lines, with war again upon us, after a few years of undisturbed peace'. But there was little that Scots accountants could do about it. 'The same tyrannous militarism has to be opposed and crushed again', it told members. 'So be it. We will prevail. And what then? Enough, for the present, to win the war, but let us, in due course, in the hour of victory, think twenty, thirty, forty years ahead, so that our sons and grandsons may not, after so short an interval, be involved again in this senseless, if manly, occupation'. By the following November it was the economic outlook which was being considered. Under the heading of: 'Shall we be ruined?' members were asked:

> *Why is it that we really dread what seems to be inevitable bankruptcy at the conclusion of this war? It is because we know that if the present process of higher and higher taxation continues conjointly*

with the present process of more and more inflation, then eventually
extremes will meet. Half the population, previously industrious and
with savings, will have no money left; and the other half, previously
spendthrift, will be earning tremendous wages worth precisely
nothing to them. Admittedly the war must be financed, and that
is a very ticklish problem; but that the national economy should be
wantonly destroyed by the way, when all previous wars have been
so economically successful, does seem a very hard thing. Cannot we
make a change before it is too late, and plan to win this war in the
counting house as well as on the battlefield?

By May 1941 an announcement that 'HM Government are appealing for a quantity of accounting, adding, and calculating machines, and also typewriters, required urgently in the offices of organisations engaged in the production of aircraft and armaments', was relayed to members. 'This appeal', it was said, 'is specially directed to those concerns whose volume of accounting routine has fallen, and it is believed that such organisations will be only too ready to sell, hire, or lend whatever equipment can be spared. The scheme proposed will allow of a quick return at the conclusion of hostilities'. In February 1944 good humour was being stretched to the limit and members were being harangued on the tough times that rationing was bringing. 'Must we submit to the loss of our self-stropping razor?', was the big question. 'Blades of the ordinary type are unprocurable. Our stand-by in time of stubble was our three-guinea, shimmering, silver box. Must we be denied even this just because manufacturers are not allowed to supply us with a baby part? Must we appear at the Appeal Court like Major General Wingate at a Council of Chindits – unkempt, uncouth, unbelievable'. And there was also the question of other parts of an accountant's uniform. 'If we cannot patch our breeks with the Hun at the gates, how shall we get on when there is no such compelling inducement to be frugal? To suggest that we might return to the kilt is, of course, most airily to beg the question'. By the turn of the new year in January 1945 a degree of weariness was setting in. 'We are subdued', said the editorial in *The Accountants' Magazine*. 'In regard to the length of the war we have been wrong and wrong again. A year ago we compared the tipping of the scales in 1943 to the favourable turn in 1917 of the last war. We thought peace or, at least, an end to hostilities, would come to Europe in 1944. We were wrong'. But, though it may have been a clutching at straws the same editorial had news of enterprise. 'It may be of interest that in 1944 we used 43% less paper than we did in 1939, but we printed only 18% fewer words; in 1944 we printed the same number of words as in 1940, but on 176 less pages. We receive few letters from readers, but we are indebted to those who write approvingly and also to the few who criticise and point out the error of our ways'. Meanwhile a review of the official Government statistics was hailed as showing 'a magnificent record'. A third of the population, over ten million men and women, were in the services, 5,700 naval vessels and 102,000 aircraft had been built. But 3,000 merchant ships had been lost, UK consumption was down by 21%, and 200,000 houses had been destroyed while hardly any new ones had been built. Government expenditure, which had stood at £1,013 million in 1938 was, in 1943, up to £5,782 million. And personal taxation now took 36% of personal incomes, as opposed to 22.5% before the war. But by June 1945 members heard that: 'The tumult and the shouting are behind us'. And the verdict? 'We can regard with some satisfaction what will probably be our improved position in Europe and in the world at large as a result of the achievements and behaviour of our troops and the moderation of our politicians. They know in France, Holland, Denmark, Norway, Greece, yes, and in Timbuktu, that we British are neither dogmatic doctrinaires on the one hand nor entirely cynical businessmen on the other. We should have influence'. One aftermath of the war was commented upon in May 1948. Under the heading of 'Usquebaugh' members learned that: 'What have come to be known in taxation as "The Whisky Cases" contain so many unusual features that their concluding stages cannot be allowed to pass unnoticed. Here, as a result of war conditions, one found two salient factors, both of which lent themselves to large-scale and easy enough tax avoidance or evasion. In the first place, there was a commodity which had increased in value a hundredfold, and the ownership of which, in the second place, could be transferred by the simple passing of delivery orders. There were, of course, the factors of its long life and immunity from decay, (apart from ullage). These circumstances were too much for certain people who sought to take advantage of the position (and, of course, the state of the law), and there followed, in the result, what one supposes must be the most prolonged and expensive tax litigation ever known in this country. Indeed, the massed ranks of Counsel and others acting for the many interested parties necessitated the removal of the hearing of the case before the Special Commissioners from the usual place of hearing to premises large enough to accommodate the unusual numbers. There has never probably been anything in the commercial history of Scotland even remotely like this episode'.

Sundries 7: Nae Enron Here

There was still scope for free thinking in the audit profession in 1944. The accounts of The Stair Society, audited by one Thomas J Millar CA, of Edinburgh, were signed off as 'Heard, seen, considerit, calculat and allowit by the Auditor'. It was a world away from Companies Acts and Sarbanes-Oxley rules.

The Glory of Summer School

The annual Summer School at St Andrews played an extraordinary role in the life of ICAS for almost half a century. From 1953 until 1996 it provided members with the chance to meet together in the most relaxed of social circumstances, to hear papers given by distinguished guests, to debate these amongst themselves and with their authors and, for those that way inclined, to take in a bit of golf. That, on the surface, was what it was about. But it developed into something else. It became a touchstone for ICAS and its membership. As *Accountancy Age* put it in 1983:

> *The point is that to sustain the value of the School, merchant bankers should sit down and talk with small practitioners from Perth and remember that they are talking to each other not out of curiosity about what each other does but because there is a perceived common purpose in being Scots chartered accountants.*

Newly qualified accountants could meet, on equal terms, with senior partners and chairmen. Many a senior appointment years later could be traced to a chance meeting years before. It was more friendship than networking and it worked all the better for that. It was a relaxed and trusting environment. Victor McDougall, when looking back over his 25 years as Secretary of ICAS at the 1976 Summer School opened his talk with the announcement that: 'Like everyone else who has ever addressed the Institute's Summer School, I reserve the right to depart at my discretion from the title given to me'. It also became a place for furious argument. On one famous occasion one eminent academic took such an affront to a critical comment at a plenary session that he packed his bags overnight and never darkened the door of St Andrews again. On the other hand such luminaries as Denis Healey, when shadow foreign secretary, thoroughly enjoyed themselves. 'I'm from the opposition and I'm here to horrify you', he told one session. Equally the social side, with the increasingly elaborate 'smoker' on the Saturday evening after dinner, grew in importance in cementing relationships and having a high level of fun. The arrival of Charlie Clark also upped the tempo. He joined the institute staff in 1984 having previously been a pipe-major in the Royal Scots. Whilst serving in the Black Watch he had been one of the nine pipers who led the cortège from the White House at the funeral of President Kennedy. There would come a point during every 'smoker', after the elaborate sketches, songs and humour, when the pipes would skirl forth and dancing would be underway. These evenings were even more taxing when the Summer School was held in June. In the early hours a restorative repast of bread and cheese and other fortifiers would be served. At this point people might have thought that bed should be their next port of call. But a glance outside at the dawn breaking usually changed their minds.

Victor McDougall, in his 1976 talk, recalled: 'How three former conveners of the Summer School and I once showed St Andrews Cathedral at sunrise to a distinguished American visitor to our Summer School and succeeded in so interesting him in the delivery arrangements in this country for milk that his re-organisation of the patterns of milk bottles on sundry doorsteps must have considerably complicated the day's chores for numerous St Andrian housewives'. But most people simply contented themselves with taking a bottle of whisky down to the incomparable stretch of beach and remarking lengthily on the many colourful qualities of the sunrise.

The golf also played an important part. There was an official tournament, usually on the Friday afternoon. But as the Old Course at St Andrews is a public course keen golfers would rise with the dawn and have played some twelve or so holes before an official arrived to charge them the green fees. And they would still make breakfast in time. Golf also created more scope for mischief. In the year of Norman

Lessel's presidency his first drive veered off at 90 degrees and clattered amongst the blades of a nearby mowing machine. By that evening, when trophies were being presented, an inventive group had bought a model mower, mounted it on a wooden stand and had an engraved plate affixed proclaiming it to be 'The President's Cutter', to be presented in future years for the most embarrassing shot of the afternoon.

The Summer School was also prone to practical jokes. One year the porters noticed that the numbers on the bedroom doors had been changed around to create confusion. They set about changing them back but found that the task was harder than they had envisaged. The numbers were stuck fast under years of varnish. Then the penny dropped. It wasn't the numbers which had been changed around. The inventive pranksters had moved the whole doors. Similarly in 1979 extensive prior research pinpointed the bedroom directly above the top table area of the dining hall below. The speeches were in full flow. But so, it transpired, were the bath taps in the room above. What started as drips into coffee cups turned into a deluge. The following year the President, David Bruce, opened a precautionary umbrella above his head before starting out on his speech. Overseas visitors, having no knowledge of the previous year's flood, thought him barking mad.

The Summer School was also a place where the politics of the wider accounting profession could be sorted out. In 1994 *The Times* reported that: 'For several years, the afternoons during what used to be known as the ICAS Summer School, when most people play golf or enjoy other leisurely pursuits, would find the secretaries of the accountancy bodies taking a stroll around the harbour at Crail, or the castle at St Andrews. The issue they were trying to resolve was that of audit regulation'.

The Summer School broke down barriers. It was the habit for the speakers to pop into discussion groups to add further insight. *Accountancy Age* reported on one such occasion when Bruce Pattullo, then Chief Executive of the Bank of Scotland, paid a visit to the discussion group headed up by the immediate Past President, Jack Shaw, himself to go on to become Governor of the Bank of Scotland. 'Tipped off that Pattullo was coming to the group Jack Shaw set about organising some role-playing to get a point across. When Pattullo arrived', *Age* reported, 'he found not a bunch of accountants deep in talk but a mock bank. The tables were turned around facing the door and three tellers sat facing him. All of them had their watches set to 29 minutes past three and all of them asked him if it would not be more convenient if he could come back on the following day. The "bank manager" was in a wardrobe, refusing to see anyone, and the rest of the bank "staff" were sitting about behind the tellers ostentatiously doing nothing. "Point taken", remarked Pattullo'. At the end of that 1984 Summer School the then President, Bill Morrison, started his closing remarks with the words: 'What a fine affair'. That summed up Summer Schools in their prime.

The First Summer School

The very first Summer School, in June 1953, was reported upon, modestly, by 'A Member'. It started on the Friday afternoon, 'although two members who had travelled overnight from London were observed making a preliminary reconnaissance round on the Old Course as early as ten o'clock on the morning of that day', and lasted four days. The pattern of a lecture, group discussions and then a plenary session was established. 'The last ritual of the day was for most a walk in the gloaming to the end of the harbour or to the golf links. It was during these meanderings that all the brilliant things left unsaid were remembered but, in the timeless serenity of the silent grey streets which had survived many centuries, the question of replacement values and all the other problems so lately hotly debated ceased, somehow, to have any significance'.

Whither the Profession? 4: Finesse

In July 1953 Angus MacBeath CA made some observations about the continuing impact of the 1948 Companies Act and the changed dynamic between a company's accountant and its auditor. 'It should be appreciated that directors may not always be able to understand accounting finesse', he suggested. 'Professional accountants will be all too familiar with the director, an expert in his own sphere, whose lack of accounting knowledge is abysmal and whose off-handedness and apparent lack of interest in the information which is required for the completion of his annual return for Income Tax and Surtax purposes drives the accountant to distraction'. He then makes a point about the understandability of accounts. 'It has been suggested', he said, 'that the public should be educated to understand accounts, but it does seem advisable that accountants should handle all matters connected with accountancy and leave others to their own pursuits, so that by maintaining high standards in the various spheres we may bring division of labour to a point where it produces the highest possible standard for the benefit of the country as a whole'.

Sundries 8: Getting Out

The journalist Jack House celebrated the ICAS Centenary in June 1954 by recalling how he had escaped from an accountancy training and taken to journalism. It was the accountancy correspondence course which started the rot. 'One evening I sat down and wrote a story of about 500 words in a little over twenty minutes', he said. 'I sent it off to Blackie's Children's Annual. Within a fortnight I had received a cheque for £1. Having the advantage of a CA apprentice's training, I worked out that, with application, I could make £3 an hour writing. And that seemed better than 10s.6d. a week'. His studies suffered. 'One day the Director of Studies of the correspondence college sent for me and said he wasn't satisfied with the way my work was going. I explained that I had something else on my mind – I'd been writing a book called "Eight Plays for Wolf Cubs". He looked at me incredulously and then said: "And has it been published?". I replied that not only had it been published, but that I had received my first royalties, and they amounted to £58. The Director of Studies then dismissed me from his presence, but I had the feeling that, the moment I was out of his office, he was going to start writing a book for the Wolf Cubs'. House's accounting career continued on its downward path. 'I was a disappointment to the partners', he said, 'and one day, on the way to an audit in Govan, the junior partner said I'd really have to make up my mind whether I was going to be a Chartered Accountant or not'. It took a matter of seconds. 'I made up my mind then and there, and lost no time in getting myself a job as a telephonist on a Glasgow evening newspaper. I gave up my bowler hat with never a backward glance, and took to wearing a dashing snap-brim, and matching ties and hankies, and other signs of decadence. And now, so far am I lost to the profession, I can't even make up a Trial Balance'.

The Second Summer School

The second Summer School, in September 1954, saw the start of another of its great traditions. 'A novel feature this year', it was reported, 'was the informal gathering on the last evening which showed signs of developing into a sort of Ceilidh'. The official account of the event was written by Bill Slimmings, later to become both President of the Institute and Sir William Slimmings, a wise and thoughtful man.

'The inaugural dinner', he reported, 'was interrupted by an urgent announcement by the President – "I understand that some eight or nine cars have been left outside without lights. I would suggest that the culprits – of whom I am one – take immediate steps to rectify the position" and he himself was taking steps almost before he had finished speaking'. Across the four days 'the papers were of a high standard, full of the raw material of discussion, and the lecturers made as good a show verbally as they had done in their written contributions'. As for the Ceilidh, Slimmings made the point that: 'At the start, the staider members might have been seen casting glances over their shoulders, as if to make sure no apprentices had sneaked in, but soon everyone, fortified by a University song-book and an extension of bar hours, was bawling the ballads that generations of students have claimed as their own. The highlight of these proceedings was a tape-recording by Mr Lang, purporting to give a Dimblebyesque report on the activities of the school – "And now we shall go over to one of the discussion groups and listen to their deliberations … 'Twist !'…". That bit of nonsense brought to an end the five days of work and play. Was it all worth while? To one who disapproves of mixing the grave and the gay, who is not content unless a clear-cut solution, however dull, is found to every problem, the answer would probably be no. To another who relished good-humoured debate, even if it hammers out only partial solutions, in an atmosphere remote from that in which he does his ordinary work, the answer is certainly yes. And we would guess the ayes had it very easily'.

Summer School: Extra Curricula

Sir David Tweedie, chairman of the International Accounting Standards Board and described by *Business Week* magazine in June 2004 as 'the most powerful accountant on the planet', was always an achiever. The Summer School held in September 1978 featured a 'Treasure Hunt on foot around St Andrews' for those not involved in playing golf on the Sunday afternoon. 'The participants found', it was reported, 'despite their enjoyment, that a knowledge of Scottish history and some familiarity with the conventions of *The Times* crossword puzzle – not to mention low cunning – helped them on their way. The erudite winners were Stewart Hamilton and David Tweedie'. And just to show his all round abilities he cropped up again in the report of the Summer School held in June 1981. 'The putting prize', it was reported, 'went to David Tweedie'.

Whither the Profession? 5: Overview

In December 1971 the esteemed Professor William Baxter, of the London School of Economics, gave a talk to London members about the development of the profession. 'It is easy to find out about such things as non-integration, new tax laws, and litigation against auditors', he said, 'but remarkably hard to discover what changes are occurring in the workaday round of the average accountant or auditor; we know about the doings of Institute committees, but not of the inarticulate members'. He attempted this task. He talked of the increasing size and concentration of accounting firms. In 1957 there had been nine amalgamations or mergers of firms. By 1966 the annual figure was up to 60. As a result he said: 'Few small firms have the resources now needed to recruit, pay, and give advanced training to young accountants; and only in a big firm can members specialise fully and so provide expertise in all the old and new skills'. But even this was under threat. 'A few years ago, every partner might be expected to cover all the client's needs: one wonders whether there are still many firms that have resisted specialisation and expect each partner to be competent in everything

– from tax to costing, and from capital budgeting to computers'. Pay was also an issue. 'The increased demand for accountants has had various results', he reported. 'One is a rapid rise in pay. Some years ago, I was startled to hear that a certain firm was luring in bright graduate apprentices by offering them as much as £300 a year. The subsequent depreciation of the pound sterling may now justify double that rate, but in fact it has at least quadrupled'.

There were other quirks which might follow from this. 'A senior partner once told me', he continued, 'that his firm was resisting high pay because austerity is essential for the moral fibre of a professional man. We must hope that a fallacy lurks somewhere in this argument too. Otherwise the moral fibre of senior partners would seem to be at risk'. He then spoke of: 'The criticism that has in the last few years been directed against accounting, both from inside the profession and from outside. Its suddenness and vehemence are remarkable; till a few years ago, accountants seemed well satisfied with their profession, and outsiders tended to treat it with respect'.

He said that there were four main targets for criticism – 'the organisation and procedures of professional bodies; training and intellectual standards; mistakes in reported profits, because of human error or inflation; and lack of standardisation in reported profits'. This latter was the topic of the moment and Baxter's concluding paragraph summed up the dilemmas well, under the heading of: 'No Sunny Future'. 'Even if all these fears prove groundless it would be absurd to look forward to a sunny era in which, thanks to standards, there will be no more criticism and we can all feel smug again', he said. 'Improvements in accounting education and new complexities such as price-level adjustment are likely to bring the publication of alternative profit figures; and these will excite ridicule. Moreover, standards cannot make us able to predict the future. Someone must still guess the size of a bad debt, the life of a machine, the outcome of difficult building contracts, and so on; inevitably some of the guesses will prove wrong, and there will be more ridicule. So we must grow thick skins. And there can in the long run be no escape from the task of trying to educate our critics. These suppose, not unnaturally, that measuring profit is an operation akin to measuring physical size, so that diverging estimates must stem from error or stupidity. Our fundamental problem is that the laws of physical measurement and of economic measurement are very different. But this is another story'.

Whither the Profession? 6: Education

In 1996 a book of essays was published to celebrate the 90th birthday of William Baxter, Professor Emeritus at the London School of Economics. One of the essays was written by Professor Geoffrey Whittington. He quoted Arthur Morison, a veteran of Thomson McLintock, writing in 1970. 'The power of free and rational argument remains, I am old fashioned enough to believe, the best road to truth in human affairs. I would therefore give companies the maximum freedom to present their accounts in whatever way they thought fit, and would then require them to explain and justify the course they had taken. The auditor's task, no light one, would be to ensure that they did. And to see that they did it fairly'. Professor Whittington added: 'It may be no coincidence that William Baxter and Arthur Morison were both trained as Scottish chartered accountants. The tradition of the Scottish profession has always been to lay great stress on the importance of independent professional judgement, and the importance of education in equipping professionals for that responsibility'.

ICAS EDUCATION, 1979-2004: A MOVING PICTURE

BY

IAN MARRIAN AND MARK ALLISON

Education is coming to be thought of as a life-long activity, and professional education is no exception. It is really quite unrealistic to talk about a person becoming 'qualified' at a particular moment, as if a dramatic change took place at that time. It is equally unrealistic to suppose that without further reading and study he could stay 'qualified' until he retires. Qualification is a continuing process, not an attainment of grace. David Solomons, 1974

A sea of change in British politics swept Mrs Thatcher and the Conservatives to power in 1979, and closer to home, ICAS was also about to change, at least as far as education was concerned.

Sir Ian Morrow had led the successful Scottish Chartered Accountants Trust for Education (SCATE) Appeal, raising £842,000 for a new education building. The Appeal was generously supported by an ICAS membership which then numbered just less than 10,000. Stewart House provided the permanent setting for Edinburgh education until 2001, and the move from Queen Street.

Twenty-five years ago, there was nothing remarkable or worrying about student performance. Ronnie Williamson, who sadly died at the age of 52 in 1978, as the Institute's first Director of Education, and then Cunnie Rankin built up and led an able team of full-time lecturers for the Institute's full-time classes. The days of Friday/Saturday classes were in the past, and ICAS was operating a block release programme in

Glasgow and Edinburgh. A three route entry scheme existed; with most students following an approved accounting degree. Some undertook a non-accounting degree followed by a postgraduate diploma, with a smaller still group entering with a Scottish HND. Most students completed their exams in 18 months. The overall pass rate for the year was 68.8% for Part I exams and 69.3% for Part II. These were comparable with the previous year's results, though not as high as the 76+% achieved in both parts in 1975. But all was not as well as it seemed and soon ICAS was to have a rude awakening.

In 1980 pass rates in Parts I and II examinations fell by over 23% and 22% respectively. What had gone wrong? Was it the calibre of the students themselves, a drop in standards by the ICAS education department or a different standard of assessment being applied by the examiners? Subsequent analysis showed that there was no single reason, but a combination of factors. It was not, as some believed at the time, due to the strain on the ICAS education department caused by a greatly increased intake of students in the late 1970s. Nevertheless, for The Working Party on Student Education reporting to Council *"the dramatic change in the 1980 results should give cause for very serious concern"*. Something had to be done.

Ironically, perhaps, 1980 was also the year of Professor David Flint's challenging report *The Impact of Change on the Accountancy Profession* (1980). He posed the question of whether enough was being done by ICAS and other training bodies *"to communicate to candidates for entry an understanding of professional concepts"*. Public interest demanded *"comparability of education, training and experience of all who hold out to the public that they are accountants"*. Clearly, David Flint envisaged a more unified profession with, for example, a common policy across the UK and Ireland for admission requirements. He was concerned about the accountability of the profession to the public:

> *How the profession is organised, regulated and governed, how its members are educated, trained and disciplined are not matters of a purely domestic nature but are matters of public concern.*

The response

Following on from the deliberations of a working party consisting of Gordon Lowden, Bill Morrison and Jack Shaw, all of whom were destined to become Presidents of the Institute, a rigorous and educationally sound scheme of education and examination was introduced in 1983. A new preliminary course and examination were introduced. Students were given four weeks of intensive teaching on three preliminary subjects: elementary taxation; elementary accounting; and mathematical techniques, before their exam which was composed of multiple choice questions only. Students were allowed two attempts at the exam within a period of three weeks and those failing at both attempts became ineligible to continue in the student education scheme. In other words it was a sudden death examination designed to stop those at an early stage who, on the face of it, were not able to cope with the basics of the profession. Contrary to arrangements for all other exams the Preliminary Exam was set and marked by the Institute's own lecturing staff albeit with external moderation as happens at the universities. Accountancy degree holders were not exempt from the Preliminary exam, a controversial decision.

Changes were also made to Part I and II of the professional exams. Rather than teach and examine each subject on a one off basis the decision was made to tackle them on a progressive basis over the two examinations. With the addition of a new subject Professional Organisation and Ethics the number of papers taken by students increased over the two parts from six to eleven!

Not content with these developments the Institute added a fourth exam to the scheme, namely the newly created Test of Professional Competence (TPC) which in accordance with the Eighth Directive as then understood by the Institute was taken after the completion of the three year training contract. This was and still is a multi-discipline case study question which over a period of five hours requires the student to demonstrate that he or she can apply their theoretical knowledge in practice.

The class contact time increased by over 30% from 16 weeks to 21 weeks, which with the higher cash cost imposed a significant extra burden on employers, and indeed on students. These substantial and not necessarily welcome changes came in over the three years starting in the autumn of 1983. They were overseen by the Education Committee chaired by Frank Kidd, again a future President, and a newly appointed Director General of Education, Ian Marrian, on secondment from Deloitte Haskins and Sells for a period of three years commencing in 1981.

The beginning of case studies

Although the first sitting of the TPC did not take place until 1986 a lot of work was required of the education department and the Examining Board. Ian Marrian and Mike Crabtree, Convener of the Examining Board and a partner with what is now KPMG, started the process by travelling to Toronto and Montreal to see the Canadian Institute's Test of Professional Competence in operation. Of particular interest was the concept of a residential marking school where groups of exam markers worked together to get consistent marking standards. In addition because of the judgement required in marking large case study scripts the concept of marking all scripts twice was noted as being essential.

On their return to Scotland Marrian and Crabtree set about developing the prototypes for the education and examining processes respectively. The examining process required Crabtree's skills as a mathematician to work out statistical means of comparing individual markers standards and finalise candidates' marks after the two and sometime three markings. The education department also had to embark on identification of real life case study material for teaching and mock exam purposes. Learning to teach in multi-discipline mode was just as challenging to the lecturers as examining in that mode was to examiners, let alone to the students about to take the first such exam.

As part of the development process the Examining Board decided to try a dummy run on the new exam format. Recently qualified members were asked to volunteer to take an all day mock exam at Peebles Hydro. In return they were offered a quality dinner, and an overnight stay with the use of the leisure facilities! Those volunteering were told that the exam was 'open book' and that they could bring into the exam any text they wished. In some cases literally wheelbarrow loads of texts were brought in. In the subsequent review of the exercise the volunteers indicated that even with five hours to take the exam there was little time to refer to the texts. As a consequence the Examining Board defined 'open-book' as accounting, auditing and ethical standards and the Tax Acts for the purposes of this exam, a principle which is still applied incidentally in 2004.

In addition to all of the above Ian Marrian noted in *The Accountant's Magazine* (1983), there would be two further important changes. First, tutors marking home exercises were to be accessible for students to meet as often as necessary, and not to be in some distant part of the UK. And secondly, "*students will be required to complete certain 'hands on' case studies on micro-computers between block I and II*". Micro-computers, no less! Investment in hardware followed and ICAS IT education led by Les Muggridge, Sandra Brown and others took off. Kit was transported around Scotland in a number of battered Volvos, and 15 years of fighting to stay ahead of hardware and software changes ensued.

Not quite right …

These changes were just part of a process which included a reassessment of how CAs could be better prepared through their education for future challenges in practice and in business. Commissioned by the ICAS education department, Niall Lothian, then a senior lecturer in the Department of Accountancy and Finance at Heriot-Watt University and subsequently a President of the Institute, produced an insightful report entitled *The CA in the 1990s - an educational profile* (1985). The decision to commission the report was prompted by the remarkable speed of technological innovation. In particular, the micro-chip was having a significant impact on the accountant's information gathering and data processing. The ICAS Education Committee had in 1984 also recognised the danger of a syllabus created by a small core of ICAS members of similar mind and background. Disappointingly, however, Niall Lothian's invitation to readers in *The Accountant's Magazine* to contribute to the project resulted in only five responses.

More members were selected for the research and, in the end, a total of 78 interviews were conducted. The report sets out a series of recommendations for change including both *"fine tuning and structural"* alterations to the syllabus (1985). Regarding the latter, specific recommendations included establishing subject-by-subject working parties and commissioning industry analysis reports. A nine month extension to the training contract was also suggested. This involved a six month secondment to an industrial, commercial or public organisation for every CA student who had passed the Part II examination.

Whilst there was a general acceptance of the technical skills of CAs there was strong criticism of the *"lack of commercial awareness"* shown by CAs in both public practice and industry. The report highlighted the requirement of the market place to have CAs who had a broader range of business and social skills. It was not an alien concept in ICAS education, and ICAS had been recruiting graduates with non relevant degrees for many years.

The problem was that, after the new initiatives taken in 1983, non accounting graduates were put off. University accounting and finance departments had also opposed the preliminary examination. There was a view that this was inefficient given that students had attained a university degree in accounting. Further, the increase in number of examination papers made the CA qualification unattractive compared to other alternatives open to non accounting graduates. Indeed there became a significant risk that non accounting graduates would study for examinations of ICAEW in Scotland.

By 1986, then, at the very time the new exams were being implemented for the first time, ICAS had to address the crisis of lower recruitment on the horizon.

"What is wrong with accountancy education?" M G Wells, 1987

The issues raised by the respected Australian academic Professor M G Wells mirrored those facing ICAS at that time:

An intelligent person with an open mind will learn very quickly on the job, and will cope with change and use it to advantage. Narrowly trained technocrats will simply become out of date; and the faster the rate of change the faster they become redundant.

Director of Education, Ian Marrian (now ICAS chief executive), by this time a permanent member of the ICAS staff working with Dr Tom Johnston, Principal of Heriot-Watt University as Chairman of the ICAS Educational Advisory Board, clearly determined that ICAS was not going to produce Professor Wells' *"narrowly trained technocrats"*.

Acting on a paper and proposals set out by the Education Committee (1987), Council dispensed with the preliminary exam. The syllabus was altered so that both accounting and non-accounting graduates could become a qualified CA within three years. To accomplish this, a conversion course for non-accounting graduates comprising of 13 weeks of block release tuition was spread over the first nine months of the three year training contract. Home exercises were linked in to the process.

A Degree Accreditation Committee comprising of academics and practitioners was formed to carry out ICAS specific reviews of accountancy degrees with a view to assessing exemptions.

ICAS had taken a major step forward in its preparation of "the CA in the 1990s". The changes had the desired effect and recruitment levels stabilised. But, as Sandy Black, Convener of the Education Committee and a partner in what is now Ernst & Young noted (1987):

> *The new education and training programme provides us with a basic academic training for the 1990s upon which we can build our future. It does not provide a final solution to education and training requirements for the 21st century.*

The early 1990s – A period of stability?

The period from 1988 to 1996 showed greater stability in terms of the broad format of the syllabus. This was important because employers and universities needed some confidence that ICAS was not going to continue to tinker and change policy. There were a number of features of the 1980s however which came to an end including in 1990 the dropping of the entry route to a training contract for holders of the Scottish HND. This effectively resulted in ICAS becoming a graduate only profession for most of the 1990s. There was still a mature entry route available followed by around 2% of students per year.

The year 1988 also saw a change over in the make up of the CA Education lecturing staff. The structure of having permanent lecturers in a team had diminished to the extent that nearly all of the independent subject experts were external consultants. The decision to rely more on external consultants had been taken in the early 80's with the objective of bringing more practical experience into the classroom. This was redressed by Mark Allison joining as the Subject Controller in

Auditing and Bernard Cooke joining as Subject Controller in Financial Accounting. Both had backgrounds from large firms and the focus of the education and those involved began to change.

The student intake of around 430 for most of the 1980s rose for a brief period to 489 in 1990 before settling back to 420 in 1994 and 392 in 1996. ICAS began to teach classes again in London in 1988 but student numbers were restricted to between ten and 20 a year, largely accounting degree holders working with Coopers & Lybrand and Peat Marwick McLintock.

Classes in Aberdeen had also begun, mostly at the somewhat surreal location of the Beach Ballroom. The rooms used varied from the ballroom itself with silver disco balls and exotic coloured lighting to function suites with views of the boats sailing in and out of the harbour. A sometimes welcome distraction for students and lecturers alike!

The fall in student intake in Scotland more generally was directly attributable to the growth in use of technology leading to efficiencies in practising offices and in client accounting systems, and most noticeably by the mergers of the large firms. The history of the large firm mergers saw a reduction in ICAS student intake of around 20 to 30 students each time. These reductions were not immediate but once the firms had re-evaluated their staffing following the merger, cut backs in graduate recruitment followed.

Industry route (TOPPs)

Recognising the falling student intake numbers ICAS looked closely at a model operating in Ireland under the guise of a training in industry scheme. The Irish Institute of CAs had managed to run a pilot scheme for a number of years where around 10% of the annual intake of students (around 50) had started CA training. ICAS devoted significant energies to trying to break into industrial, commercial and public sector training routes through contacting senior members in all areas of the profession and some interesting new training places were unearthed. These companies, known as Training Outside Public Practice (TOPPs), were accredited in the same way as other training organisations and students followed the same route in terms of attendance at classes and examinations. The maximum intake from this scheme never represented more than 5% of ICAS students. The reasons for this were complex but the movement of many plc headquarters from Scotland to London (and resulting training decisions) together with some very strong schemes run by other institutes notably CIMA, meant that the wish to change was often low.

Accounting degrees

The 1988–1996 scheme did see another interesting trend develop in that the percentages of students with a fully accredited accounting degrees (81% in 1990) had dropped to some 70% by 1996. The majority of these non accounting degree students were employed by the large firms. It was clear that employers in Scotland began to see that a broader intake might be to the benefit of their business needs, even if those students had little or no knowledge of accounting at date of commencement.

Teaching

The teaching side had changed to a model of full-time ICAS staff, one looking after each of the syllabus subjects. This resulted in a larger team at Rowan House in Glasgow than had been seen before, headed up by John McDonagh; a permanent London Training Manager in Neil Smith, now a Director with Deutsche Bank; and Derek Allen, still Director of Tax, devoting more time to tax education. Although there were many stalwarts amongst the continuing external lecturers few students in the 25 years will forget the insight and humour of the

Glasgow tax mafia, Tommy Docherty and Bob Harris. Both brought their experiences with clients and dealings with the Inland Revenue and Customs and Excise to the classroom in a manner which brought the subject alive.

The final year classes continued to be largely the preserve of external consultants bringing in their wider business experience to the case studies. The material creation and innovative delivery designed by the likes of Richard Wrigley, Stephen Grant and Colin Garvie kept ICAS material current and relevant throughout the 1990s and developed the early model in a unique way.

ICAS had found that arranging for regular and timely commitments from partners and employees of large organisations was difficult. What was needed was a core group of part-time lecturers who had the time, skill and interest to marry ICAS involvement with "real life".

Richard Wrigley brought his droll Yorkshire sense of humour, and life of running a Glasgow practice to the creation and delivery of many finance and multi-discipline case studies.

Stephen Grant used his Stirling practice and knowledge of industry and ICAS to develop management and multi-discipline case studies.

Colin Garvie had a healthy disdain for audit and financial reporting, but his insight and experiences for raising and managing cash contributed to excellent case studies.

Others including Andrew Dobson and Murray Steele brought experience from industry and practice, whilst Ian Fraser and Willie Henry added solid teaching skills to interest in financial reporting and auditing.

Last of the big bang reviews

The Education Committee Conveners of the time, Andrew Hall, at the time a senior executive with Shell, and Kirsty Gray, a partner with Moores Rowland, had overseen a period of relatively constant education performance with stable examination pass rates. However Council asked the Committee to carry out a major review of the syllabus in 1994. This review was driven with an eye on recruitment numbers but also on the usefulness of the syllabus to members after qualification. Elizabeth Gammie, a lecturer at Robert Gordon University together with Mark Allison, by then Director of Student Education, carried out this work which was presented both to the ICAS Education Committee and to the IFAC Education Committee in 1995. The research showed that member needs post qualification in some areas were different to those being delivered by the CA qualification. The Education Committee and other ICAS working groups then developed a number of proposals over a period of two years to address these issues. These proposals included:

1. options appearing in the qualification;

2. the development of a Technician qualification;

3. a review of work experience and the student Log Book;

4. the merging of mathematical techniques and economics into the rest of the syllabus; and

5. a dedicated syllabus in the final year Test of Professional Expertise.

In education terms these were radical suggestions and Council was concerned that ICAS may have taken too long in the process to arrive at them, and thereafter implement them. As Robert Smith, the 1996/1997 President, noted "in education and training, the clear consensus across the spectrum is that ICAS should maintain the process of continuing review of the relevance of the qualification to changing needs". One practical aspect of this was that there would no longer be major education reviews carried out every five or six years. Instead the syllabus and all aspects of education were required to be reviewed annually. To help to achieve this and oversee change in education generally, Mark Allison was appointed Director of Education, with far wider responsibilities than previous incumbents.

The options debate

The consideration of options in 1996–1997 was not the first time ICAS had debated the issue. At the end of the British Institute considerations in 1989 ICAS had developed a proposal of nine specialisms, students being required to attempt one alongside their multidiscipline case study. After market research this was rejected by Council. The second occasion resulted from the Gammie/Allison research and on this occasion five optional papers were developed. The Education Committee were at pains in this development to ensure that this was not seen as specialisms but rather as options to reflect what students carried out in the workplace. There was significant support from most commentators for this development but at the last minute Council requested a change of direction and the extra papers were rejected.

The principle, however, of ICAS attempting to assess relevant workplace experience was accepted and ultimately led to the development of a more flexible form of student training record, the Achievement Log. The Achievement Log research concentrated on competencies expected of newly qualifying accountants. The HR assessment approaches of the large firms, some medium accounting firms, and a range of employers in industry and commerce were considered. It was decided that ICAS should merge some of the features of the old student Log Book (quantitative and narrative record) into a system of qualitative responses audited by the students' employer. This approach to competencies was not in a true sense a vocational qualification but was an application attempting to tie ICAS requirements to the needs of the workplace, rather than the other way round. Students were given the opportunity to log specialisms and options relating to work that they had had the opportunity to carry out during their training contract. This approach has been under review again in recent times but it is interesting to note that other major institutes have referenced the development of the ICAS Achievement Log to their own competency maps (Canada, New Zealand and more widely IFAC).

The options debate remains on the table but there is still a very strong view that the CA qualification should mean one thing and one thing only.

Technicians and non graduates

ICAS had been a sponsoring body of the Association of Accounting Technicians since the early 1990s. However the ICAS CA education programme did not allow for such students to enter into a training contract (in that they did not have a degree). There was concern that the Accounting Technicians in Scotland were not fulfilling the needs of employers and a consultant, Diane Walters, together with Ian Marrian and Raymond Pennie, carried out research to assess whether ICAS should set up its own Technician body or review its relationship with AAT. This latter course was taken and the Accounting Technician qualification was reviewed against the ICAS syllabus. A number of exemptions were offered and a new route was launched in 1997 which permitted full members of AAT to be eligible to train as CAs. A joint venture between ICAS and AAT ensued with full-time staff in Scotland responsible for marketing and supporting AAT employers, colleges and students. This venture continues and provides an important bedrock for Technician students in Scotland.

Other ventures

The AAT joint venture was not the only linking with another body during the 1990s. ICAS and the Association of Corporate Treasurers (ACT) entered into a very successful joint venture, only coming to an end after ten years in 2003. ICAS used its training and examining expertise to provide ACT with an education programme and examinations in accounting related disciplines.

The Chartered Institute of Public Finance Accountants (CIPFA) and ICAS started a reciprocal membership arrangement in 1996 whereby exemptions were offered to each other's qualification. This had led to as many as 20 new entrants a year joining the CA programme with a number being successful, and becoming full members of ICAS, in addition to their CIPFA qualification. A few ICAS members have taken the opportunity to follow the route in the opposite direction. The Chartered Institute of Taxation (CIoT) and ICAS formed a similar agreement in the late 1990s offering ICAS members exemption from certain CIoT papers and *vice versa*.

One line of ventures so far rejected is the opportunities available to ICAS to link up with a university business school in the delivery of an MBA. The Education Committee did review this regularly throughout the decade but for a variety of reasons always rejected the proposition. It is interesting to note that less than 2% of ICAS members have actually chosen to follow an MBA from all those that are offered throughout the world.

The challenge of 2000

By 2000 the student intake sat at 397 (90% of which were in Scotland). 70% of these students had accounting degrees with 82% having an honours degree in some discipline. This latter statistic was a result of many years of reduction in students following an ordinary degree only, as employers required an honours degree as an entry point. Even five years previously 30% of ICAS students had an ordinary degree. By 2004 this has dropped to less than 5%.

ICAS trends and operations were thrown up in the air in 2000 by the opportunity presented by Ernst & Young to create a bespoke UK wide CA education programme. The rigour of the ICAS syllabus with its solid technical hurdles was seen as attractive to the firm but a more innovative delivery model was required. ICAS Directors Mark Allison and Luisa Robertson were instrumental in creating a unique programme for Ernst & Young in conjunction with a new joint venture partner, BPP plc. Ernst & Young decided to train all their UK students with ICAS.

Soon after this, ICAS and PricewaterhouseCoopers developed a model which allowed the firm to match different training programmes to business needs and led to a further jump in CA student intake. In 2001, KPMG Tax Business school worked alongside the ICAS education team to create a further training scheme this time tying together the breadth and quality of the CA qualification with specialist tax qualifications.

ICAS had offered only one qualification delivery model up until that point (block release) and one of the requirements of these firms was that ICAS made a move towards running intensive programmes. The syllabus had changed little in the preceding years beyond some further movement of the Business Management subject matter around the syllabus and some minor changes to assessment. The changes this time therefore were on delivery and on commercial relationships rather than on content and assessment.

The immediate result of these developments was an increase in the student intake to 881, rising further in 2001 to 997. These figures represented an all time high in the Institute's 150 years and although they have fallen back to around 720 by 2004, still represent a period of tremendous challenge for the education and examination teams. A new Qualification Board was set up in 2000 and devoted much of its early activity to overseeing these delivery changes. Brian Davidson, a partner in PwC, both convened the outgoing Education Committee and then the new Qualification Board for a total period of six years and his wise counsel on the practical needs of large firms were a very important part of the process. Latterly Douglas Nisbet, a partner in Ernst & Young, has taken over this important strategic Board.

Assessment

The ICAS Examining Board has had to react to the periods of change reflected in many of the comments in this chapter. It has done so at a time of many challenges to ICAS and the education function in a way which has continued to maintain the standards expected of the qualifying Chartered Accountant. Ronnie Sinclair, a partner with Chiene & Tait, convened the Board during the early 1990s handing over in 1999 to Professor Pauline Weetman. Professor Weetman had been involved in the numerous changes to the methods of examining Financial Reporting throughout the 1990s and latterly saw through the transition of the main technical level of examinations (Test of Professional Skills) to a model involving the Education staff. The Examining Board exists as a standard setter and control mechanism to the many varying inputs from syllabus content, through delivery, to materials, and student intake. Jim Gibson has taken on the role of Convener of the Examining Board and its running of the final entrance exam from 2004. Strong links now exist between the examination function and education in a more official capacity, but in truth these have existed well throughout the 1990s with a close relationship between the Convener of the Examining Board and the Director of Education. These links are also now formalised with the Qualification Board including two members of the Examining Board.

However the Examining Board rightly continue to jealously guard their full independence and reporting line to the Institute's Council. A recent development has seen the first lay member appointed to the Board.

Europe and international

The CA Education function within ICAS has not only had to consider Scottish and UK changes but also consultancy opportunities which have arisen, and changing regulation even now in the area of education coming from both the EC and more widely IFAC.

The consultancy opportunities arose in many former Soviet Union countries following the fall of the Berlin Wall and saw ICAS Education staff working in Russia, Kazakhstan, Romania, Poland, Czech Republic, and also in Africa and further afield in New Zealand and Hong Kong. These consultancy opportunities continue to place the ICAS Education model internationally.

On the regulatory front the IFAC Education Committee issued in 2003 the first six International Education Standards. These now present a challenge to ICAS to comply with, and there are others in the pipeline. Undoubtedly the way ahead will see more regulation and influence from both Brussels and New York.

Joint education initiatives between ICAS sister bodies and in new groupings formed around the European Union have produced education sharing initiatives and projects with long term common goals. To date none of these initiatives have resulted in many implementable outcomes but these continue to be an opportunity for benchmarking the ICAS qualification against others.

The next 25 years

The ICAS strategy review in 2003 set its horizons at 2010. Looking beyond that is difficult and truthfully the speed of change in the last five years shows that predicting even as far as 2010 is full of flaws. Undoubtedly regulation will provide a greater challenge than it has done in the last 25 years. The move to mandatory CPD will bring a number of years of research and innovation. Many members already operate in an environment with an enlightened outlook towards personal learning and development. Others would like to but have found in the past that their work – life balance has often set training and development to one side.

The method of education will continue to evolve. It will always need to be moulded and shaped in harmony with a continually changing external environment. The *status quo* is not an option.

A much greater proportion of CAs will train and qualify outside of Scotland. The sense of identity and belonging to the Scottish Institute that has characterised the attitude of many CAs that were trained in Scotland, will not be as prevalent in the future. What can ICAS do through its educational outreach to make sure that all students and CAs qualifying outside of Scotland feel proud to be a member of ICAS?

Finally, public confidence in the profession will remain a key issue as long as major corporate failures, through fraud or negligence continue to come to light. The ethical dimension to education, combined with sound and informed professional judgement, cannot be ignored.

It has been said that film-makers became the most important historians of the twentieth century, for better or for worse. The public perception of historical figures and events has been strongly influenced by the images on the big screen. Less dramatically but arguably more importantly, individual and corporate reputations, and by extension the livelihoods of thousands of people, are dependent on the integrity and professionalism of trained accountants. The public often perceive that it is the fault of the accountants when businesses fail, thanks in no small part to the major recent corporate failures of Enron, Andersen, Parmalat *et al.* It is a moving picture, however, and it is the ongoing challenge for ICAS to educate and train accountants of the highest ethical and professional standard, so that the public can continue to have complete confidence in all who carry the letters CA after their name.

Ian Marrian is Chief Executive and Secretary at ICAS and was Director of Education 1984 to 1995. Mark Allison has been Director of Education since 1995.

The Distaff Side 6: Looking Back

In September 1977 Beatrice Moore CA, provided some insight into the lot of a woman trying to become an accountant in the 1930s. Many firms simply would not take her on at all.

However, Thomson McLintock & Co., with commendable foresight and comforting faith, accepted my application, so that in the autumn of 1937 I became their first female apprentice for several years. There had been others before me; some had even stayed the course and qualified; but others had fallen by the wayside when their health broke down or the exams proved too much. But I had no doubts about my ability to succeed. So I joined the staff under the able tutelage and kindly interest of H E Borland, one of the partners; and, although I never worked directly for the senior partner, J P Dowling, he had great faith in me, spurred me on in the face of all opposition, guided my path, and right through his life took a personal interest in my progress.

She described how in the audit room:

There were long, vehement discussions on religion, philosophy and other serious and unrelated subjects, in between which I managed to learn a great deal about bookkeeping, auditing, accountancy, trusts, bankruptcies, liquidations and many other aspects of the profession. We worked from 9 till 5.30 and our classes were held after work and lasted for about two hours. There was no day release, and we were not permitted to study Scots Law in preference to Mercantile Law, as the classes for the former were in the morning and would have necessitated absence from work. Neither did we get time off before exams to study, although I think when exams fell at the end of a week we were granted leave of absence for the earlier part of that week.

These were happy days, when we had one Saturday morning off per month, but on the Saturdays we were "working", all repaired to the Grosvenor Tea Room for coffee, and if we were working out during the week it was customary to have coffee there en route. These were the days when a first-year apprentice earned £20 per annum rising to £60 in his final year; but there were still firms in Edinburgh where, far from receiving a salary, an apprentice had to pay a premium to his firm in return for his apprenticeship. Being a girl in what was then a male-dominated profession had some problems, especially where clients were concerned. Care had to be exercised as to where I was sent, as not all clients would tolerate, let alone welcome, the female of the species to audit their books. Initially a few eyebrows were raised, and a certain air of suspicion prevailed, but after war broke out that attitude changed, and businesses welcomed anyone with the expertise to check books and produce reliable accounts. Nevertheless there was then and, in some cases still is a lack of complete faith, a vague suspicion that the "lady auditor" was second best.

The Centenary Celebrations

In June 1954 the Institute celebrated its Centenary with church services, dinners, a conference, golf matches and even motor coach tours to the Borders. The Institute Secretary, Victor McDougall, in an article in *The Glasgow Evening Times*, pointed out that:

*A century ago there were 97 CAs, all in Glasgow or Edinburgh. Today there are more than 5,600 of them. Half of the 5,600 are in Scotland. The rest are elsewhere in the United Kingdom or in 71 other countries. This is why the Institute's name is The Institute of Chartered Accountants **of** Scotland and not the Institute of Chartered Accountants **in** Scotland.*

Some 2,000 people took part in the celebrations and, according to *The Accountants' Magazine*, 'the joy and good fellowship that they all so evidently felt created an atmosphere which assured the success of the celebrations and which everyone who took part is likely to remember for a long time'. It started with a sherry party at the President's house and continued the following morning with a service at St Giles' Cathedral. 'The day was grey, but did not deter attendance', it was reported. The message from the sermon was: 'Keep your heads cool, and your hearts warm. Think hard and speak soberly. Avoid all hysteria, whether of optimism or pessimism'. A Presidential luncheon followed. Then it was on to the Usher Hall. Here the President, Sir John Somerville, reminded the 1000-strong audience that:

> *We are celebrating the centenary of the oldest existing body of accountants in the world and some of our guests have been good enough to say that they look upon this occasion as the centenary of the modern accountancy profession, in the foundation of which Scotland led the world.*

In the evening a dinner for some 492 people was held at the Assembly Rooms, though the report says that 'the number who desired tickets was greatly in excess of the number of places available'. A fine 1949 Burgundy followed by Pol Roger champagne from 1943 helped wash down the 'Tranches de Saumon du Tay'. In the speeches a Past President of the American Institute, Loyall McLaren, made the traditional point that 'Scotland has sent out its sons to the four corners of the world' and that 'in the country we call America no single group has been more important in developing our modern business life than the blood which we so proudly claim as part of America today that comes from Edinburgh and from Scotland'. Sidney Mearns in toasting 'Our Guests' referred back to the menu of the 1904 dinner which celebrated the Jubilee of the Society of Accountants in Edinburgh. 'Those halcyon days', he exclaimed, 'when men were free, when hydrogen bombs and consolidated balance sheets had not been invented; when income tax had just moved, in a forgivable graciousness, from eleven pence to a shilling in the pound; and when the cost of living, Gentlemen, believe it or not was no more than half-a-croon a bottle – best quality three-and-saxpence'. The tenth, and last, speech of the night concluded: 'Well, gentlemen, I think I have said enough. The hour is very late. I understand there is a certain amount of gambling going on as to whether we would finish at 11.30. I would sit down now, hoping that all our guests have had an enjoyable time here'. You might wonder how enjoyable the Ladies' Dinner, which was taking place at the same time just up the road at the Adam Rooms, might have been. There were no speeches but after dinner there was a film show. They watched a film about the Scottish Highlands, one of the recent Royal Tour of New Zealand, and a third illustrating the tweed and wool industry in the Border Country. After all this excitement 'there followed a patient wait until the Banquet concluded and the gentlemen arrived with cars to take their ladies home'. Such were the joys of 1954.

The following day was the Centenary Golf Competition, which after the lengthy previous evening, was surprisingly won by the President. Meanwhile 'ladies, guests and apprentices and their ladies' were involved in motor coach tours around the Borders. Even here the rigorous application of accounting was observed. 'Each coach', it was reported, 'was accompanied by an apprentice who ensured that the number of persons on board when the coach moved off after a halt was no fewer than it had been when the halt was called'. In the evening a Civic Reception took place and Edinburgh Castle was illuminated from 10.30 until midnight in honour of the occasion. The following day, in plenary session, two papers, one on the history of the profession and the other on the future of the profession were given. There was then another Presidential Luncheon and a lunch for Lady members of the Institute, at which due thanks were paid to 'those members who were the first to accept women as apprentice chartered accountants'. 950 people then attended the Centenary Ball at the Assembly Rooms. As if this was not enough it was reported that similar Centenary dinners were held in Calcutta, ('where songs were sung until the gathering concluded at midnight'), Cape Town, Colombo, Johannesburg, Montreal, New York City, (where the main course was described as 'English Mixed Grill'), Salisbury in Rhodesia, (where they had obtained a haggis), and in Suva in the Fiji Islands, where, being on the international date line, the first toast to the institute's second century was given.

Victor McDougall's Own Quarter Century

When the Edinburgh Society, the Aberdeen Society and the Glasgow Institute decided to amalgamate in December 1950 they also decided to appoint a Secretary to run the newly united ICAS. Quirkily they chose an Englishman from the Law Society in London. They can have had little idea of quite what a far-reaching decision they had made. Victor McDougall ran ICAS from 1951 until 1976 and exerted much influence on the profession for years after. This is what Robert Bruce wrote in *The Times* when Victor died in October 1998:

When Victor McDougall took up the post of Secretary of the Institute of Chartered Accountants of Scotland in 1951, there were only six members of staff. And he was pleased to tell you that his job had previously been done by another six practitioners who had provided their services voluntarily in addition to their responsibilities to their accounting firms. By the time that he retired, in 1976, the accountancy profession had been transformed. And his role in the coming of age of the profession and of the politics of its complex relationships was immense. Victor McDougall was also a very gregarious and entertaining man. Last week, at the age of 87, he died while mowing the lawn in his quiet Edinburgh garden. He first came to Edinburgh at a crucial time. The main Scottish accountancy bodies had just combined to create the ICAS. So his 25 years at the helm were genuinely the years that forged that body's pre-eminence among accountants. It might have seemed an odd post for him to take. He qualified as a solicitor in 1933 in London and worked at the Law Society from 1938. He was largely responsible for the administrative work in creating the system of legal aid. He was very proud of that and furious at its demise last year. His author's notes to an article that he wrote in December last year read: Victor McDougall, who was the Law Society's under-secretary, legal aid, on the introduction of the civil legal aid scheme in 1950, never expected to live to see its demise – and certainly not by fiat of a Labour Government.

That shows his style clearly – loyal, determined and very much aware that barbed wit wins more battles than technical submissions. Victor McDougall was a big man whose eyes were full of fun and who, with his wife Gwen, greatly enjoyed all of his activities.

When one of the more lively founders of the Sixties hippy movement wrote his memoirs, it might have surprised some of the staider Edinburgh accountants that Gwen and Victor McDougall were among the book's dedicatees. However the two of them put much effort into sorting out the disastrous financial affairs of the chaotic arts scene in Edinburgh. It was part of a wide social life.

Victor always claimed that he had "too much Scots blood, on both sides, to feel comfortably English, yet not enough to feel comfortably Scottish". However, it was his defence of the Scots belief that, being the oldest accountancy body in the world, it should also have a fair claim to be the finest, that triumphed. It was typical that when he wrote a history to update his own centenary history of the Institute, he would rub the point in by calling it The Fifth Quarter-Century. In that, he said "'Scottishness' is not just the clash of passionately held views on the right tactics to follow in any particular situation. It involves something deeper – things such as the recognition of members' pride in belonging to the oldest existing accountancy body in the world, and a concern for education and training, for a high-standing professional qualification, for quality rather than quantity in both students and members, for emphasising the importance of individual professional judgement, for seeking, particularly in the international field, to understand and reason with people who hold different points of view".

No wonder he relished the politics that grew as the UK's six accountancy bodies took part in the astonishing growth of accountancy as a profession and a career from the early 1960s. He knew more than anyone about the problems of trying to merge accounting bodies. Referring to the 1969 proposals, he wrote: "Stated thus, the proposals may sound simple enough. A moment's thought should, however, dispel that illusion. The broad ideas were inevitably clogged by a mass of 'nitty-gritty'". When accountancy bodies were arguing over merging this summer, he took a similar view.

The last letter that I received from him was full of cogent, forthright and occasionally scurrilous points of view. He suggested an article on the current merger activity. "I would be happy to discuss a more detailed and less undiplomatic approach to the matter" was the way that he put it. Victor loved the daftness of the politics of people. He would clutch his huge hands together and his eyes would disappear in great smiles of delight over the foolishness of people trapped in the profession's politics. He was a very mischievous individual.

On retirement he delivered a paper to the Institute's Summer school. In it, he concocted a timechart showing world events alongside those of the institute. Juxtaposition of "revolution in Russia" with "first golf competition for the Moore Cup" was typical. However, he also produced the sort of thorough examination of the profession that is rarely attempted 20 years on. And in it, he summed up the lessons. One of them was: "Changes resulting from mature thought by good leaders are usually a good thing; changes dictated by fear are usually a bad thing". And then he added: "Many fears thought to dictate changes are groundless anyway". Wisdom and wit, as Victor knew so well, are the only way of making sense of the world'.

Newfangled 7: Uncommunicative

In December 1954 the problems of business communication were coming to the fore. 'One of the early tasks of the accountant in industry is to cultivate what has been called the art of meaningful communication', members were told. 'Very few accountants are naturally endowed in this respect'. What the accountant needed to do was 'to get inside the minds of his staff and his colleagues'. Furthermore he 'will require to be simple, brief and definite'. There are warnings about the effects of jargon. 'His main objective must be that his words should be clearly understood without a mass of supplementary explanation. It is surprising', the author concluded, 'how effectively accounting instructions can be given without mention of either a debit or a credit'.

Sundries 9: *Ecurie Ecosse*

In August 1956 members were celebrating success on the sporting field. 'Congratulations to Mr David Murray CA, of Edinburgh', read the notice, 'who has brought renown to Scotland by entering the winning car in the annual international sports car 24-hour circuit race at Le Mans. This victory in a classic race is all the more splendid as

Ecurie Ecosse, Mr Murray's team of Jaguars driven by Scottish drivers is a strictly amateur concern. It is the first time since the war that a privately-owned car has won this race'. The writer then decided that a bit of a patriotic boost was in order. 'We are beginning to think', he continued, 'that when interesting things happen it is not only in Scotland but also abroad that there is likely to be a CA somewhere in the picture'.

Sundries 10: Rock 'n Roll

The rock and roll years appear to have arrived in Edinburgh later than elsewhere. Members' attention was drawn to a recent article in *The Guardian* newspaper in June 1961. It had 'lent prominence to the sociological enterprise of a group of CA apprentices in Edinburgh'. 'We imagine', it continued, 'that, although the teddy-boy problem is generally recognised, many people in Edinburgh would, like ourselves be surprised to hear that an organised band of these youths, calling themselves the Jacobites, exists in this city'. A number of CAs were, it transpired, running a youth club tailored to these Jacobites, called the Blue Door Club. As a result of violence 'the lighting is set high and the containers for the soft drinks sold are of cardboard'. The Institute approved of the scheme. 'The young men who run it confirm our belief that CA apprentices are not in any way behind their masters in the range of their interests and achievements', it noted.

Sundries 11: Trusting

In August 1961 members heard the tale of 'The Threepenny-ha'penny Van'. It sounds like the title of a children's story-book for the under-fives, but it is fact, not fiction, and no fairies entered into the affair at any time, we believe. It happened in Musselburgh, known as the Honest Toun, a small town near Edinburgh. A local garage proprietor wished to find a new home for a ten-year-old GPO mail van which he had been trying to sell and which was in good running order. He decided to sell it for the nominal sum of three and a half pence. He advertised it by chalking the price on it and driving it in a local gala day procession. In spite of the maximum publicity thus achieved he received no offers. Although six people enquired about the van, such was their innate caution that none of them would believe that the offer for sale at such a price was genuine. It took an accountant apprentice aged 19 to weigh up the financial risk involved and, contrary to public opinion of accounting caution, to venture the sum of three and a half pence in making a firm order. The van was his without delay. To judge from a photograph in the local press, notwithstanding a front mudguard patch that seems to have been *sewn* on, he must have got a bargain, even by Musselburgh standards.

Whither the Profession? 7: Looking Ahead

An extremely youthful D P Tweedie CA contributed an article to *The Accountants' Magazine* in October 1975. Then he was a lecturer at Edinburgh University. These days he is Sir David Tweedie, architect of a global system of financial reporting as Chairman of the International Accounting Standards Board. In 1975 he was writing about 'The Corporate Report', the ground-breaking report into how attitudes should change relating to users of accounts. Tweedie argued that it had dealt with the issue of providing a package of financial information to a wider audience. But he argued that it had not addressed the issue of creating 'a more appropriate system of income measurement and asset valuation' – themes which Tweedie is still, almost thirty years later, hammering away at. His conclusion was that 'The Corporate Report' was 'a stimulating attempt' to find an answer to the question of communicating the information. 'However', he concluded, 'while we contemplate the possible revolution in the company's accountability, it is imperative that the accountant's method of communicating quantitative and qualitative information should evolve, so that the full benefits of change may be enjoyed by the wider audience the proposed corporate report is intended to reach'. Plus ca change.

Newfangled 8: Baffled

A great breakthrough was announced in May 1959.

The Institute of Chartered Accountants of Scotland held its first Computer Course at the Marine Hotel, Troon, Ayrshire, from April 15 to 18.

It was clearly felt that the Institute was onto something here. 'Those taking part numbered 110; a further 51 members who applied but for whom it was impossible to find places on this Course have been offered priority bookings for the second Course which it is planned to hold in mid-October'. The course had started on the Wednesday evening with a 'showing of films on computers'. On the Thursday there was a session on 'Computers Available in Britain', on Friday on 'Advantages of Electronic Data Processing'. All this culminated on the Saturday morning with a 'visit to a computer in operation at the IBM factory at Greenock'. It was reported that:

For long periods in many of the sessions one could have heard a punched card drop; sometimes the silence might have been interpreted as baffled stupefaction at some piece of almost incredible information, but most of the time as absorbed interest. One suggestion was that learning to talk the new computer language was like passing the sound barrier – difficult to achieve and resulting in somewhat uncouth noises.

Whither the Profession? 8: Inflation

In April 1977 the great battle over an appropriate method of accounting for inflation, at a time when inflation zigzagged around in double figures, was still being fought. It was down to Professor William Baxter, of the London School of Economics, to provide some sense in an increasingly feverish debate which had added to the public perception that accountants knew their technical arguments but didn't have any practical answers to serious problems. The proposed solution about which the argument revolved was a document called ED 18. 'The sad thing about ED 18', said Baxter, 'is that it mixes so much good with so much bad. On assets and costs, it is good; on income, it is bad. If it is pushed through as it stands, the bad parts may do enormous harm to accountants and accounting. A bad concept may seem innocuous from afar, but when applied is apt to kick its user in the teeth'.

Whither the Profession? 9: Metaphorically

The arguments over proposals to provide a method for accounting for inflation had by November 1977 been reduced to semantics. Professor William Baxter, of the London School of Economics, had produced an article arguing that both the proposed systems, current cost accounting and current purchasing power, were flawed. A lecturer at

Dundee University provided some support. 'It does not seem entirely fair to refer to this paper as *Accountancy Age* did with the headline: "Baxter floats last ditch inflation compromise". Entirely apart from the dreadful mixed metaphor, it is wrong to use the word "compromise", which implies something less perfect than either alternative'.

Whither the Profession? 10: Dearing

In January 1989 the regulation of the profession was the topic of the moment. The profession had asked a leading civil servant, Sir Ron Dearing (later Lord Dearing), to produce a report on 'The Making of Accounting Standards'. It was to lead to the current regulatory system based on a Financial Reporting Council.

The Accountant's Magazine ran a wonderful leader column on the report under the heading: 'Do, Do, Ron, Ron'. Amongst the gems it said: 'The report is interesting, novel and imaginative – to quote three Civil Service forms of abuse. Written in a polished, moderate and stylish manner, the report reflects the nature of its author, whose commitment to his task ran even to designing the cover, which shows, appropriately, the words "True and Fair" over and over again as a background to the title.

The cynics might say that the report removes from the professional bodies their authority for setting accounting standards while committing them to an open-ended, four-fold increase in costs; that it introduces decision-making related to accounting standards in five fora, (the Financial Reporting Council, the Accounting Standards Board, the Emerging Issues group, the Review Panel and the courts); that it therefore creates a new and rich seam of work for lawyers and imposes on company directors a liability for a new statutory declaration and a new civil offence for failing to comply. But wait a minute. Didn't the submission to Sir Ron from several bodies, (including our own), press for more autonomy for the standard-setting body amongst other things, and for a reduction in its size? Is the profession not becoming more litigious anyway and is there not an existing criminal offence for failing to comply with the Companies Act requirements for accounts?'. In the end the conclusion was that if the professional bodies 'now have a tiger by the tail, they have only themselves to blame'.

A learned article in the same issue had this to say in conclusion: 'The scene is set then for a period of great importance for the profession. In the Dearing Report it has an excellent foundation on which to build. Sir Ron Dearing's committee was not afraid to confront the issues head on; so too must the profession as it attempts to implement the proposals. It cannot afford to fail. If it does, then it will find its critics and its rivals all too ready to seize the initiative. That may require serious soul-searching. And while it will require some short-term sacrifices it should also enhance the profession's long-term standing and importance within the financial community'.

Changing the Lines of Responsibility: The Journey From Self Regulation to Regulation by Government

By

Nigel Macdonald

The story of how self regulation was replaced by statutory regulation is interesting, not merely because it reflects major changes in how government has come to see the economy and from the interaction with the EC, but also because it has impacted directly on ICAS's own independence as an institute. Coincidentally the change affected financial services and audit at about the same time, although the drivers for change were very different. The realisation by the ICAS Council in the latter part of the 1980s that disciplinary controls over the membership would largely be replaced by controls over firms, of which the largest would be regulated by ICAEW, was a major factor in its decision to explore a merger with that body, a proposition subsequently rejected by the membership.

So what really happened to bring about these changes? The financial services story is the most interesting, because it was entirely UK driven, whereas the audit changes stemmed from changes forced by the EC.

The early years of the Thatcher government were characterised by serious economic difficulty, but the challenges were not an accident. One of her administration's deliberate intentions of removing exchange control at the very beginning of that term had been to expose the commercial sector to the full force of international competition, for that was the market in which it had to survive and prosper, and the advent of North Sea oil might cushion the shock of the adjustments required. British industry suffered very seriously as a result, although the survivors became far stronger as a result of the experience.

One result was that it became clear to all, including the government itself, that the nation's prosperity was critically dependent upon the success of 'UK financial services plc', covering the whole banking, insurance and financial services sectors, and that manufacturing strength alone was never going to be sufficient to maintain the country's economic strength. Although the 'invisible earnings' statistics showed that the financial sector had been contributing successfully to the economy as a whole, exchange control had sheltered that sector too from the full effects of international competition. A further challenge arising was that by the early 1980s the EEC was broadening its focus from competition in products and services markets to bringing down the barriers which had previously limited competition in capital markets as well. This coming change represented a challenge and an opportunity for the City of London and 'UK financial services plc' more generally which needed to be faced 'head-on'.

The key areas that could threaten success for the sector in the European and international markets were identified as transaction costs, the risk of fraud that could threaten the integrity of the market, and of course effective regulation of the financial markets themselves.

To offer the lowest possible transaction costs needed much more than a rapid move to computerised dealing; there was no longer room for both jobbers and brokers to make a margin, and the simplification of the dealing structures that resulted in 'big bang' was a pre-requisite for the changes needed to ensure that London could offer the lowest possible transaction costs.

To minimise fraud the accountancy profession's senior member, Lord Benson, (who as Henry Benson had long led Coopers & Lybrand) was commissioned to carry out a review which led to numerous legislative changes, including changes in insolvency law requiring directors to maintain systems that allowed them to be informed as to the state of the company's affairs at any time, and making it a criminal offence for directors to mislead auditors. The review also stimulated a review by the profession as to whether the obligations on auditors to find fraud were sufficiently clear, and fresh guidance resulted. The Serious Fraud Office was also established at this time to give more focus to the need for enforcement.

Regulation of the market prompted a number of changes, for the previous somewhat piecemeal oversight arrangements carried out by the Department of Trade and Industry, the London Stock Exchange and by the Bank of England, needed fundamental restructuring as part of the creation of the new Securities and Investment Board and subsequently the Financial Services Authority. An important shift also took place in the 'centre of gravity' of regulation as a result of the Financial Services Act from the previous position where the DTI took the lead, supported by those bodies (with the Bank of England liaising closely with HM Treasury), to the current position where the Treasury exercises oversight of the whole financial market *via* the Financial Services Authority. Tripartite responsibilities for auditors of banks and building societies were introduced, to provide direct channels of feedback to regulators. The subsequent failure of BCCI (which was not 'caught' by the new regulatory structure and tripartite arrangements because it was registered in Luxembourg rather than in London) highlighted the importance of such new reporting arrangements.

As part of the wider changes the Financial Services Act introduced a requirement that anyone offering financial advice must be regulated, to ensure that they took proper account of the financial situation of the individual concerned, gave appropriate advice, and that where they purported to given independent advice (as opposed to being the tied agent of a larger concern) they had indeed explored the market properly. The regulation was to be administered *via* the trade association relevant to the type of financial services offered, for example life insurance or independent financial advisors, within the relevant sector of the financial services market. Naturally the buying and selling of shares in listed companies was covered, but so was advice about buying or selling blocks of shares in unlisted companies. Many accountants had been providing such broad financial advice as part of their everyday business or occasionally, and so found themselves caught by the legislation.

The question arose, was this activity by accounting professionals of sufficient materiality to warrant a separate regulatory regime? The government aim was to introduce a sensible compromise – where the activity was relatively minor it would be overseen by the profession itself, on behalf of the regulators, where material the activity would be registered as a separate activity and regulation would be administered by the relevant trade body. The dividing line was originally drawn around the question, "was the main business of the firm carrying on the profession, or not?" As a consequence, in the initial stages some significant corporate finance work was authorised, along with discretionary investment management and advice on and arranging transactions in "securities" where this was not the main business of the firm. Subsequently the test became whether each transaction/ advice in question was incidental to another professional service that was not investment business. Provided the services offered were likely to be incidental in this way the firms could register with their designated professional body (DPB) for that business and were then exempt from the need to obtain separate authorisation from the FSA. The test was then "incidentality" on a transaction by transaction basis, but this still allowed some very substantial transactions to be carried out – particularly in relation to private company corporate finance work.

As a result the profession's role had to include not just maintaining a registration record of firms and individuals carrying out such activities, but also monitoring the activities of the member on a sample basis, (together with recommendations for improvement where relevant) and providing regular formal feedback to the regulator as to the maintenance of standards with withdrawal of registration where standards fell seriously short. Thus even without the audit regulation arrangements described below, coming into effect at almost the same time, formal monitoring procedures were required along with registration procedures. A joint monitoring unit was established which carried out that work for the three bodies together. By acting jointly in this way the potential for competition between the DPBs for registration of firms was – effectively - eliminated. Whilst they may have looked like self regulation to the average practitioner, these monitoring arrangements were in fact agency arrangements carried out on behalf of others by the members' own professional body, and at the member's expense.

Audit regulation has a much longer history, stemming right back to the introduction of legislation requiring that that all companies be audited and that only suitably qualified individuals be deemed competent in law to carry out an audit. For many years that meant simply that the individual concerned had to be a chartered accountant, and as a result the institutes fulfilled the role of regulator, through education and training, and through investigation and discipline in those few cases where a member was thought to have acted improperly. For many years however it was much more common to be removed from membership for failing to pay a subscription than for anything connected with unsatisfactory auditing.

But the background of compulsory audit for all companies together with a large and active capital market in which the legal requirement for audit was supported as a sensible way of reducing the risk of misleading financial information, which lay behind the responsibilities and freedoms of self-regulation enjoyed by the accountancy profession in the UK, were not the norm shared in most other countries of the world. One of the early objectives of the EEC (reflected in the 4th Directive) was to introduce some commonality into the way companies were required to report on the financial affairs, and it was not until the 8th Directive that the Commission felt able to introduce proposals requiring auditors to be regulated in some way, where they had responsibility for reporting on company affairs. Indeed it had been the case that in some European counties audit was overseen by finance or economic ministries, in others it was seen as the primary responsibility of departments of justice. The 8th Directive introduced some useful clarity, recognised the importance of audit for larger companies as essential to the maintenance of orderly financial markets and required explicit responsibility to be taken by governments. It also triggered the change that we have seen in the UK in recent times removing the obligation for audit for smaller companies, for there was no such existing obligation elsewhere in the EC and the 8th Directive did not introduce one.

In the UK the oversight responsibility was assumed by the Secretary of State for Trade and Industry and consultation took place as to whether the government itself should regulate the accountancy profession, or operate a delegated powers regime that the 8th Directive also allowed. The latter route was chosen, and, like the regime for financial services, this required the profession to set up procedures for audit registration, monitoring oversight and on occasion removal of the right to audit, all under the delegated oversight of the DTI. The monitoring regime was carried out alongside the new joint monitoring regime for financial services, and because many ICAS members worked alongside members of the ICAEW or ICAI, a significant benefit of the joint approach was the application of common methodologies and approach for the whole sector. Each institute conducted its own delegated audit regulation and registration procedures, under the continuing supervision of the DTI, but joint policies and procedures were maintained though an ongoing programme of co-operation between the bodies.

Naturally, as experience was gained, the monitoring process evolved. The benefits of a risk-based approach became clear and systems allowing effective desk-top monitoring of annual returns, coupled with proactive investigations, were introduced successfully. Once all practices had been the subject of at least one monitoring visit the basis of selecting firms was reviewed to reflect the risk based approach and increased emphasis was also placed on the underlying methodologies and control systems in place in the larger firms. That evolution is expected to continue with increasing focus on the way audit opinions are formed so as to be able to better assess the quality of such opinions.

The joint monitoring arrangements continued until the end of 2003 when, in anticipation of the new regulatory regime under which audit monitoring responsibilities will fall to be carried out by the Public Oversight Board of the Financial Reporting Council, and financial services monitoring by the FSA, ICAEW ended the joint arrangements with the other bodies. ICAS introduced practice review in anticipation of these changes, which has been well received by those taking advantage of the service, and the other institutes are either doing the same already or are considering doing so.

The new audit monitoring regime that has been established by the Public Oversight Board is not exactly the same as that operated previously under the joint monitoring arrangements. In the initial stages at least the new board is adopting a risk-based approach to monitoring and is thus confining its monitoring activities to major listed companies and will later extend its review to all listed companies. However it is understood that the board may further extend its role to monitoring major unlisted companies and may wish (subject to establishing the legal basis for doing so) to extend its review further to such organisations as public interest charities and possibly even to other non-corporate public interest entities. So, for the time being at least, the Institutes retain some responsibilities for audit monitoring.

Regulation presents significant problem for governments as well as for the profession. Whilst it is not the purpose of this short summary of the profession's journey from self regulation to regulation by government, to act as apologist for government, it must be recognised that in a consumerist society the concept of *caveat emptor* finds little public sympathy. Regulation is a response to that pressure, but governments do not enjoy the financial exposure and consequential budgetary pressures that result from finding themselves called on to act as effective guarantor of the probity of the financial sector. Governments are fully alert as well to the risk of financial exposure as a result of a major audit failure, and the apparent 'arms length' structure of the Financial Reporting Council and the ongoing monitoring role of the public oversight board is no accident, despite the government's considerable influence over the policy and workings of those bodies. In this context it is salutary to remember that responsibility for audit registration still lies with the Institutes and that they might be first in line (not the Financial Reporting Council or the FSA) in the event of another major audit failure.

Nigel Macdonald is Convener of the Research Committee and was ICAS President 1993-1994.

Sundries 12: Rugby

March 1970 brought an unexpected triumph on the rugby field. 'It is no infrequent occurrence to have a CA or a CA student in the Scottish international rugby team', it was noted, 'but in the victorious match against England on March 21 at Murrayfield, (the Calcutta Cup), there were both. Peter C Brown, who played at number 8, is a member of the Scottish Institute and John N M Frame, (playing at number 13), is a CA student. Both have been capped before and both had a good match, Peter Brown in particular being described in *The Scotsman* as "the life and soul of the party"'. It was reported to members that: 'The final score was Scotland 14 England 5, and the match, which also included a brilliant try scored by England, was justifiably described by an (English!) BBC commentator as "sumptuous"'.

The Old Rivalry

In May 1899 some remarks at the annual general meeting of the Institute of Chartered Accountants in England and Wales provoked fury and contempt from north of the border. The President of the day referred to parliamentary efforts 'on behalf of the Scottish Chartered Accountants'. The President stated that 'the Council were not prepared to assent to the passing of the Bill which, whilst placing no restrictions on Scottish Chartered Accountants coming to and practising in England and Wales, would practically have prohibited a large majority of members of the English Institute from undertaking business in Scotland. "It is absurd", said the President, "to suppose that our members, on the remote chance of obtaining some business in Scotland, would prepare themselves for, and submit to, an examination by the Scottish Institute, supplementary to our own; and it is obvious that our clients, in the event of our services being required, could not be expected to wait until we had the opportunity of proving our efficiency in Scots law'.

The Editorial in *The Accountants' Magazine* which contained this report was unequivocal in dismissing this example of English equivocation.

That he completely misrepresented the attitude of the Scottish Societies towards English Accountants practising in Scotland will be seen by any one who takes the trouble to refer to an article in our July number last year … . The same fallacy has repeatedly appeared in other quarters and as often has been exposed.

So that was that; until the dastardly English got uppity again.

Sundries 13: The Birthright

A letter appeared in *The Times* in December 1971 asking what the Race Relations Board might make of an advertisement from a Scottish accounting firm which the writer had seen a few years previously.

Scottish Accountants have vacancies for Apprentices wishing to train as Scottish Chartered Accountants

it had read.

Training open to Englishmen seeking to acquire by diligence what they missed at birth.

Nothing New Under the Sun

The idea of merging the competing accountancy bodies in the UK into one body is not quite as old a concept as the bodies themselves – but it goes back a long way. On Friday 19 January 1900 George Auldjo Jamieson, who had been President of the Edinburgh Society from 1882 until 1888, spoke at the second annual dinner of the Scottish Chartered Accountants in London. The report of the event in *The Accountants' Magazine* said:

> *... that he looked forward to a great growth of the profession of Accountants, from the well-known energy of Englishmen as well as Scotsmen, and he trusted that the idea of a better understanding between the professions in both countries, which had been referred to, would be realised; that there might be an amalgamation of the Chartered Societies, and that thus the prospect might be furthered of a complete assimilation of the laws of England and Scotland. The present diversity was an absurdity which he ventured to say would before the close of the twentieth century have passed away.*

In March 1903 the great pioneer of Scots accounting, George A Touch, who had yet to add the 'e' to his name to create the great Touche accounting brand which would reverberate down the subsequent century, was talking mergers again at the fourth annual dinner of the Association of Scottish Chartered Accountants in London. The report in *The Accountants' Magazine* said that:

> *He hoped the Joint-Committee of Chartered Accountants which had been formed would remain in office until such time as they had an actual federation of all the chartered societies. He felt sure that the Committee would take no narrow, or parochial, or provincial view of the situation, but that they would approach it realising the fact that*

accountancy, like anatomy, was much the same all the world over; and he hoped they would direct their energies towards the federation, not only of the societies and institutes within the British Isles, but of the Colonial institutes as well.

The Certainties of the Past and the Problems of the Future – The Profession's Merger Battles 1965-1989

BY

Robert Bruce

In 1989 a bitter battle was fought. For some the result was seen as the triumph of the independence of Scots accountants. For others it was seen as a failure to grasp destiny and expand Scots influence on an increasingly international stage. It was the attempt to create a British Institute.

But to understand how such a concept came about you need to go back to the late 1960s, and also to understand how the idea of a federation, or amalgamation, of chartered accountants had been a potent idea since the nineteenth century. Logic has always appealed to people running complex structures, and accounting bodies are nothing if they are not complex structures. In February 1900 you could find a Past President of the Edinburgh Society from 1882 suggesting that 'the present diversity was an absurdity' and that an amalgamation of the scattered accounting bodies was inevitable, eventually.

It is the argument about that concept of 'eventually' which has kept the idea of merging accounting bodies into one on the drawing board. As Victor McDougall puts it in his history of ICAS from 1954 to 1979, *The Fifth Quarter Century*:

> *In the early 1960s there was a strong case for doing something about the organisation of the accountancy profession in Great Britain and Ireland. The only question was – what should that something be?*

There had been a complex series of manoeuvres in the early 1960s between various of the bodies. In 1965 the ICAEW had proposed that the certified accountants, the cost and works accountants, precursors of today's CIMA, and the municipal treasurers, precursors of today's CIPFA, should join them. ICAS was not asked. But the ICAS council did debate the idea of joining in and rejected it. 'The conclusions were inevitable', wrote McDougall.

> *The ICAS must retain its influence and independence; yet it could not afford to stand aside, since if the ICAEW were to swallow up all the members of the other three London-based bodies as Chartered Accountants the ICAS position in Scotland itself, quite apart from the rest of Great Britain, would be seriously threatened.*

The answer was simple. A scheme whereby the three chartered accountancy institutes, English, Scottish and Irish, swallowed up the members of the other three accounting bodies and would then work 'harmoniously together as a united accountancy profession' was put forward.

The devil, as always in such plans, was in the detail. 'The problems', recounted McDougall, 'were found to be almost awe-inspiring in their complexity. They were tackled with skill and devotion, by members and staff from all six bodies. Looking back', he concluded, 'one should not be surprised that the resulting plans were complicated, largely misunderstood by the members generally, and a failure'.

It was decided that each of the six bodies should vote on whether to proceed with detailed schemes of integration. 'It was soon evident within the ICAS', said McDougall, 'that opinion was bitterly divided. Moreover there were signs that some members had neither read nor understood the proposals. Older members felt less affected by the proposals than did the younger. Some of the latter argued fiercely that their "birthright" was being sold to people from other bodies who had not made the sacrifices – educational and financial – that they and their parents had done to secure for them the CA qualification by hard work rather than gift'. All four bodies other than the ICAEW and ICAS voted overwhelmingly to proceed. The ICAEW almost had the two-thirds majority it needed. ICAS members voted 50.5% in favour, 49.5% against. It was deemed that ICAS had approval to proceed but not necessarily the authority. In theory it was felt ICAS should pull out and as the result of a previous agreement between all the bodies the whole integration scheme would founder. But the other five bodies reneged on that deal. They wanted to go ahead regardless of the Scots.

There were several crisis-ridden months for ICAS. The President, Sir William Slimmings, suggested that the change of tack of the other five bodies created 'a situation different from that on which the referendum was held'. It emerged that quite a number of members who, having voted against the original proposal, now disagreed with the idea that ICAS should stand aside aloof from the new situation. A further vote of the membership was taken on the question:

If the English scheme is to be implemented, should the Scottish scheme be implemented at the same time?

The ICAS Council unanimously recommended it should and members, by 77.7% to 22.3%, agreed.

But it was to be of no avail. In the summer of 1970 when members of each of the six bodies were asked to vote to approve the integration agreement it was the ICAEW which came unstuck. ICAS members had voted 74% to 26% to go ahead. But instead of the majority it had achieved in the previous poll 55% of ICAEW members voted against. 'Thus ended in apparent failure', reflected McDougall, 'the united efforts which so many people had made over a period of more than five years to create a new structure for the accountancy profession in Great Britain and Ireland'.

But there were, he suggested, 'two glimmers of light on a dark horizon'. The first was that the ICAS Council felt it now had a closer rapport with the membership and the second was the idea, put forward by ICAS, that a Consultative Committee of Accountancy Bodies be created 'for consultation on matters of common interest'. This body, having had a sometimes trying history, still exists.

Speaking at the London dinner in November 1970 the President, George Dewar, said that 'during the integration debate our Council was once described as a group of peevish, frightened, tired old men who were afraid to face the challenge of the future, far less shape it. I disagree', he continued. 'The policies developed during the last few years will continue. The broad objectives of these policies are:

- to participate jointly with the other accountancy bodies in everything which affects the profession as a whole; and

- to continue our policy of advancing our education and training and thereby to continue to turn out accountants who are second to none anywhere in the world'.

He summed it up by asking: 'What assets do we have?', and summing them up as: 'A lively, intelligent membership; a first-class secretariat service; a student body in training which gives every cause for confidence in the future', and, 'our native wit and energy'. His final question was: 'And the liabilities?'. His answer to that was disarmingly honest. 'Well', he said. 'We shall need some more money sometime'.

McDougall drew three lessons from the debacle. The first was that people do not vote for proposals which, however idealistic, do not bring them direct benefits. Second that 'the more comprehensive and carefully structured in detail the grandiose proposals are the greater is the difficulty of getting them understood by the electorate'. Third that different bodies with different cultures and histories can still work effectively together without losing their identities. All of these came to the fore when the next attempt to rationalise the profession came about.

In February 1987 the lead story in *Accountancy Age* revealed that: 'Moves are afoot to resurrect the idea of unifying the UK accounting profession'. The trigger was the European Eighth Directive which, amongst other things, sought to regulate auditors. If, as it was anticipated, this raised the audit threshold and reduced regulated audit firms to a relatively small number of firms, mostly within the membership of the three bodies of chartered accountants, then it might make sense to regulate them through one merged body, much as had been planned back in the 1960s. Certainly the then ICAEW President thought so. And so, it was plain, did the Department of Trade and Industry. But Victor McDougall, a decade after retiring as ICAS Secretary, thought not. 'Accountants should ask themselves if they would like to see the powers of the six chartered bodies reduced in the ways suggested. If not they should encourage the leaders of the bodies to resist them'. The threat to ICAS was a simple one. If the market was reduced to the larger firms the majority of those firms would probably register with the ICAEW rather than ICAS.

The battle lines were drawn. Certainly, Norman Lessels, the incoming ICAS President, thought so. In an interview with *Accountancy Age* at the beginning of April he said that his personal view was 'that an outright merger would be unlikely to find favour with the members of my institute generally'. In May *The Accountant's Magazine* urged ICAS members to keep an open mind: 'Since the certainties of the past can be the problems of the future'. It said that: 'The public interest lies in maintaining effectively and demonstrably the highest standards of professional work. To that, in Scotland, must be added a recognition of Scottish cultural and historical distinctiveness. But Scottishness is not enough and never should be'. And it warned that if it came to a vote: 'That vote should be founded not upon an ill-defined nationalism but upon a well-informed and rational analysis of all the factors at work'.

Through the summer the pressure grew. Government ministers warned that the accountancy profession had to integrate. The senior partners of what were then the 'Big Eight' firms put together an informal grouping 'to speak for the profession'. By the time the traditional ICAS Summer School came around the secretaries of both ICAS and ICAEW were in full discussions, not of mergers, but just how the institutes as they stood were going to cope with the tidal wave of regulation which the Government was intent on pushing downward onto the profession. And in November a letter was sent to all members of the ICAEW and ICAS telling them that a joint working party was to be set up to examine 'the scope for exercising certain of the responsibilities undertaken by the institutes on a unified basis'. 'The key point about the working party', said the leader column in *Accountancy Age*, 'is the character and style of its two chairmen. It will meet in both Edinburgh and London. Bill Morrison and Eddie Ray, both Past Presidents of their respective institutes, will chair the proceedings. Both are men of great understanding, humour, patience, common-sense and a clear view of the practicalities. Both prefer to heal wounds and strive towards a healthy future. If anyone can succeed in this difficult task they can. They should be given all the support that is possible'. The leader in *The Accountant's Magazine* in December echoed this. 'In agreeing to the formation of the working party the Council of the Institute was clear that full account was to be taken of the Scottish dimension to the profession', it said. And concluded:'There are heavy hitters on the working party and when the time comes for their report to Council one can confidently predict that, in members' interests, the need for change will have been firmly gripped'.

The first riposte arrived in the correspondence columns of the next issue of *The Accountant's Magazine*. Ewan Brown, of merchant bankers Noble Grossart, wrote:'I know a euphemism when I see one and I saw several that concerned me in the letter to members from the President. (1) "restructuring of the profession" – first step, collaboration with England and Wales; next step, merger proposals; (2) "developments within the profession" – Scotland is in danger yet again of being dictated to by London; (3) "exercising responsibilities on a unified basis" – descent into muddled compromise or, equally dangerous, the view of the majority will always prevail; and (4) "full account was taken of the Scottish dimension of the profession" – enough said!'

At this stage no idea of merger was officially being discussed. The working party was simply exploring ways of working better together. But the idea of a hidden agenda is an attractive one. As *The Accountant's Magazine* put it when the report of the working party was finally published in May 1988: 'Treachery will be perhaps the least virulent quality ascribed to some by others'. Certainly the difficulties were plain. The ICAEW Council approved the outline plan unanimously. The ICAS Council, taking note of a furious campaign waged through the Scottish press after the report had been leaked, decided that even after devoting a whole day to their debate they were going to have to reconvene a week later in an effort to reach a conclusion. *The Scotsman* newspaper had, after all, announced that 'the death knell has sounded for the oldest accountancy body in the world'. The ICAS Council were not going to take that lightly.

The report considered a range of ideas including a federal structure or just simple improved co-operation. But it made it plain that these would not provide major benefits in terms of cost-savings, greater efficiency or speaking with a unified voice. So it was the dissolution of both the ICAEW and ICAS and the creation of a new body, a British Institute to supersede them, which the report advocated. This would be set into motion, assuming a positive vote, in 1989 with final completion in 1993. It envisaged an 80-strong Council made up of 15 Scots, 50 English and 15 co-opted members. Presidents and deputy Presidents would be elected by a nominating committee of twelve, three from

Scotland. The headquarters would be in London, administrative work would be conducted from Milton Keynes and Edinburgh would run education, teaching, research and IT services. There were signs that the creators of the report had leaned over backwards to assist acceptance by the Scots. Proportionate to their membership numbers the Scots had the advantage on Council and a Scottish College was offered to consider specifically Scottish issues and to have a considerable degree of independence. The report also went to considerable efforts to claim that it was not advocating a merger of the two existing bodies but the creation of an entirely new, British, Institute.

The ICAS Council finally voted to take the proposals forward and allow a joint constitutional committee to prepare recommendations which would go forward to a membership vote. Frank Kidd, who had only just become President, declined to give the exact voting figures from the ICAS Council vote. Long after these events he made it plain that the whole British Institute issue had seemed to him to be a hospital pass as he took up his Presidential year of office.

The Accountant's Magazine ran an editorial entitled 'The head *versus* the heart' which encapsulated the real issues for most members. 'Heartwise, as they say, no one enjoys considering, supporting or promulgating what can be seen as the end of the Institute. That feeling is intensified when it is linked to perhaps one of the most strongly developed senses of national identity in the world. But the history of mankind is littered with the victims of nationalism. This is not to deride a basic, sociological or psychological feeling of great intensity but to remind us that the latter part of this century may not be the best time to major on the maintenance of barriers. The creation of a new *British* body will give Scots members a chance to influence how things are done in a *British* way directly and with much greater impact than that possible under rapidly approaching problems'. It concluded that:

> In this most crucial of debates let us control the heart with the head
> and not simply use the head as a battering ram.

In the following month's issue Bill Morrison, as joint–creator of the report, had this to say:

The argument is not in the short term related to money. Of course, it is possible to say that we will pay whatever it takes to have a full-blown Institute going it alone, or we will cut our operations to match what we are prepared to pay. That is not the point. The point for the Scots is to preserve long-term influence in the profession of chartered accountants and it is inevitable, on a go-it-alone basis, existing and past levels of influence and participation would dwindle in the longer term, with serious future consequences for recruitment and membership. The structure of the profession and the extent of regulation have already pre-determined that.

In September the dissident opposition in Edinburgh produced its views. Professor Tom Lee of Edinburgh University made it plain that opposition centred around two areas. The first was that the proposals existed only to cater for the needs of the large accounting firms as they look less and less for 'skilled accounting technicians and increasingly for personable generalists in commercial matters'. His second was that the proposals would destroy the idea of a profession of individuals rather than firms. 'It will not be a body created to maintain the interest of individual chartered accountants. Instead it will be a trade association of firms which offer a wide range of financial services, only some of which will be accounting-related'. Meanwhile Frank Kidd started his 29 meeting campaign to put the proposals to members. *Accountancy Age*, sounding rather disappointed, reported that 'there was little of the expected hostility'. Frank Kidd was reported as saying that 'many who attended had yet to be persuaded'.

By September when the Kidd roadshow had reached London the opposition group had given up plans to issue separate proposals. Ewan Brown suggested that the issue of regulation could be solved by the creation of a joint monitoring and regulatory unit and the rest of the reasoning behind a merger, which he described as 'a cocktail of defeatism, centralism and self-interest', be scrapped. The debates continued furiously at the Summer School in the same month. The trio of Tom Lee, Ewan Brown and Ian Valentine of Binder Hamlyn had made a presentation to the previous week's Council meeting and then been told that Council 'had heard nothing new or nothing that had not been previously considered'. But Summer School at least allowed everyone to blow off steam. 'The 1988 Summer School', reported *Accountancy Age*, 'may well be seen as a key step in the process of deciding where the future of ICAS lies. Everything is now out in the open. Facts and figures have been discussed by those who care most passionately about the institute'. The paper also reported on 'the unlikely sight, on the final night of the school, of the English President and Secretary being roundly cheered for their performance of a variety of impromptu limericks'. John Warne, the ICAEW Secretary, in particular, came in for praise of his key rhyme of 'fair scunnered'.

By the turn of the year the pace of events was picking up. In the first week of January 1989 an opinion poll showed that only 24% of Scots were in favour of the measures. And the ICAS Secretary, Eric Tait, announced that he would resign from the end of May. 'He felt that plans for his future were insufficiently firm', as Frank Kidd put it. Tait told *The Accountant's Magazine* that:

> *Those opposed to the proposals for the British Institute may derive some consolation from my decision. They could not be more wrong. I firmly believe that the terms set out by the Joint Constitutional Committee are in the best interests of all members of the Institute.*

On 12 January the ICAS Council voted 17 to 8 that the proposals should go forward.

The Tait resignation was another turning point. The politics of what might happen if a British Institute came to pass were likely to be complicated. Senior figures in the English profession felt that they had been out-negotiated in the original talks and that the Scots had gained a far greater voice in the final structure than their numbers warranted. Equally, as the senior partner of one of the Big Eight firms put it: 'The best outcome would be a merged body but run by the Scottish secretariat'. The feeling that the Scots ought and would be the dominant force in the proposed new body made it politically harder to be seen to make further concessions, like guaranteeing a senior role for the ICAS Secretary ahead of the vote.

In February the final proposals were published. The role of the Scottish college had been enhanced and the Scottish subscription, being higher than that of the ICAEW, would be lowered, the designated letters to be used by qualified members were to be the Scots 'CA' designation. The two distinctive approaches to teaching would co-exist for the time being. But overall the full proposals provided a mass of detail but little change in the overall principles. The final vote was to be on 6 June.

As the date approached tempers grew shorter. But wise men appeared on all sides. *The Accountant's Magazine* ran an editorial in April entitled: 'It's now or never – part 1'. 'The proposals for a British Institute are entirely business driven', it suggested. The thesis was that with the new regulatory landscape recognising firms rather than individuals the larger firms would, over the course of time, register with the ICAEW. 'Month by month the realities of this basic shift in authority become more marked', it said. And with that dilution of allegiance many parts of the ICAS business, particularly in education, would suffer or dwindle away.

In May *The Accountant's Magazine* ran the second part of its 'Now or never' thesis. Its conclusion was:

The terms are without doubt as good as ICAS could ever get; indeed a number of ICAEW members feel that they are overly and unreasonably generous; nothing like them will re-emerge in, say, five years time. It's now or never if the Scots want to operate in the mainstream of the profession.

A new opinion poll was said to show votes moving the ICAS way. And in mid-May the veteran Past President from the previous merger battle, Sir William Slimmings, then in his late seventies, made his feelings plain. In *Accountancy Age* he referred back to the merger battles of the past and stressed that co-operation rather than competition was the way forward for the profession. 'I appreciate the deep feeling against the merger', he said, 'but I do think they are looking at it in too blinkered a way'. He was scathing about the idea of loss of influence. 'There's talk of Scots being in the minority on the proposed council', he remarked, 'but that's the wrong way to approach it. If 15 Scots cannot make an appropriate noise in a Council then there is something wrong with those Scots'.

The leader column in that issue of *Accountancy Age* had this to say:

> *It is people who matter. Among the people who drew up the proposals on the Scottish side were several Past Presidents who have been amongst the most dynamic and loyal of Scots accountants in recent years. With the growth of the international accounting firms and with the expansion of international businesses and industries, the UK profession, when it comes to the ordinary members, has already merged. Scots, English, Welsh, Irish and increasingly, other Europeans, all work together. The proposals going to the June vote recognise that there are pressures from the Government's growing regulatory demands and elsewhere which make a British institute an almost inevitable method of organisation. But that should not be the point. Ultimately unless a country and its economy look outward rather than inward then it is doomed and deserves its decline. The same is true of its professions. You can argue over the merger details. But*

the final decision should be on the larger issue of how far and how wide the profession's voice should be heard.

As if to underline that point the following week saw the announcement of a merger between what was then Ernst & Whinney and Arthur Young, one of the oldest of the remaining firms with a Scottish ancestry. Other mergers were to follow.

The day of the vote came. The most prominent of the rebels, Ewan Brown, turned up wearing a union jack bunnet, which he assured everyone was not a sign of a change of mind, but a bet which would result in a donation to charity. In London the English vote was overwhelmingly for the idea with 94% in favour. In Edinburgh, on a 60% turnout, 45% were in favour and 55% against. It was not a landslide but it was decisive. And a long and heartfelt battle was over. The strategy review group which ICAS had prudently set up in January, just in case, put forward its proposals at the following week's Council meeting. Fighting off calls for his resignation the architect of the new proposals, Vice-President Ian Percy, announced that:

The proposals are radical. I am very confident that the Scots institute will remain a strong and influential body.

By December *The Accountant's Magazine* was running leader columns entitled: 'The listening Institute'.

It may have been a case of heart over head. But in the historical context it was always going to be difficult. Scotland as a whole felt aggrieved in the late 1980s. It had been used as a guinea pig for the poll tax which eventually brought the Thatcher administration down. Devolution, independence and a new Parliament were in the air. Within the profession there was a feeling of antagonism towards the big accounting firms, which were seen as starting to operate their Scottish offices as mere branches with many fewer partners rather than the strong independent units that they had been in the past. It was the smaller firms giving a kicking to the large firms. Members outwith Scotland were fiercely proud of the independent heritage of ICAS. The Scottish economy was starting to decline. There were many factors behind the result.

In *The Times*, when another doomed effort at mergers within the various London-based bodies was being mooted some four years later I wrote that: *With hindsight, the British institute proposals were lost because they coincided with a wider tide of nationalism which culminated the following spring with the Scots winning the rugby "Grand Slam" in a welter of flags and choruses of "O Flower of Scotland". Against that tide, accounting and political logic was always going to limp in second with studmarks on its hands.*

Robert Bruce was Editor of *Accountancy Age* from 1981 until 1990 and Accountancy Editor at *The Times* from 1992 until 2001.

THE CA BRAND

BY

PETER JOHNSTON

In the months leading up to the June 1989 merger vote, it became clear to the leadership of ICAS that there was significant opposition among members to the proposed merger of the three institutes of chartered accountants in Britain and Ireland and that there was a strong possibility that the merger proposal might be rejected by the Scots. In response to this, a working group was established to develop the strategy for ICAS. In the subsequent vote, some 55% of the ICAS membership voted against the proposal, which was strongly supported by members of the other two institutes.

There is little doubt that the main factor leading to the 'No' vote was concern that the unique identity of ICAS and its members would be lost if the three sister institutes were to merge. Alongside the obvious consideration of relative size of the three bodies, were pride in the collegiate spirit of ICAS and the very high value which members placed in their professional designation of 'CA'. This collegiate spirit was seen as flowing from the relatively small membership base and from the ICAS requirement that all students must attend lectures in the Institute as part of the educational process. ICAS had always been able to call upon its experienced members to pass on their skills to students in the Institute's lecture theatres and the membership valued this element of their education very deeply. There was deep disappointment on the part of those ICAS members who had supported the merger proposal and anxiety about the future viability of the Institute. They were also concerned that the leadership of the ICAEW might take the view that there was no future in further co-operation with ICAS and that they might even take retaliatory action in response to the vote. To their great credit, both the ICAEW and the ICAI accepted the position and continued to collaborate with ICAS as it made new plans for its continuing independence.

The centre piece of the new ICAS strategy was a document entitled "The Way Forward", which was published at the beginning of the year 1990 under the presidency of Professor J P (Ian) Percy. It contained the strategy for ongoing independence. The document laid down the action necessary to consolidate and build upon the reputation and standing of ICAS and the CA profession. Emphasis was firmly placed on the need for the highest standards in the main areas of education and training, practical research, technical skills and balanced, effective regulation.

As part of this process of consolidation, market research was carried out, to establish the level of awareness among other professions, business and the general public of ICAS and the CA designation. In tandem with this, a consultant was retained to advise on the future of the Institute's professional journal, *The Accountant's Magazine*, affectionately known as 'TAM'. In round terms, this research revealed that both ICAS and CA were known and recognised by those who had frequent contact with the Institute and its members, but that other professionals and the wider public were much less familiar with them.

The advice of the consultant, supported by surveys of its readership and advertisers, was that very fundamental change was required. The title and content of *The Accountant's Magazine* was seen as being worthy, but very narrow and of little interest to advertisers and the outside world. To many, it was seen as earnest, but dull and of interest only to some practitioner members and those in academe. It was clear that the journal, as it stood, was not communicating effectively with the majority of members or with the outside world.

In the light of these findings, the decision was made to launch a public relations and marketing campaign to develop both the ICAS and the CA brands and to re-launch the journal under the new title, *"CA Magazine"*. The aim was that *CA Magazine* should reach out not only to the entire membership of ICAS, but also to outside stakeholders and other interested members of the public. As part of this drive for more effective communication with members and the outside world, a central services department was established. This department employed existing and new skills in marketing and design to upgrade in-house and external publications. Members of staff of this department also provided full design and production support for *CA Magazine*. Similarly, responsibility for the design and production of a new style annual report was subsequently assumed by ICAS staff and the Central Services Department later developed the ICAS website.

It became clear that, although the ICAS and CA brands were inextricably entwined and interdependent, a different approach was required to develop them to maximum effect.

ICAS, with the status conveyed by its Royal Charter, its objectives and its Achievement of Arms, bearing the motto *Quaere Verum,* represented the dignity and probity of a body of highly respected professionals. ICAS and its membership had a long and distinguished presence in and beyond the worldwide profession. ICAS was globally recognised for the quality of its education, research and technical output. ICAS represented "the shiny badge" of its members.

The CA designation also had this dignity and probity, based upon the high value of the qualification itself and the long established global reputation of individual members. But the CA brand was also seen as having significant marketing potential as a communications medium to potential high quality students and outside stakeholders and as a merchandising tool for ICAS, its members and a radically redesigned magazine, with much broader readership appeal.

The need for care was demonstrated by a misfire in the early days of the re-branding initiative. The President and Chief Executive of the day readily accepted the kind offer of a CA, who was the finance director of a leading Wellington boot manufacturer, to produce two pairs of bespoke Wellington boots bearing the ICAS Achievement of Arms. The aim was ultimately to offer such boots for sale to ICAS members. The two pairs of excellent quality boots were duly presented. Sadly, news of this reached the ears of the Lord Lyon, who took the view that this was an inappropriate use of the Achievement of Arms. The project was immediately abandoned, although the two unique pairs of boots are still worn with pride and discretion.

Subsequent offerings, such as CA branded headwear, sweaters, ties, golf umbrellas and the like did not encounter such difficulties. Visiting colleagues and friends from sister institutes around the world eagerly accepted them as gifts and Charlie Clark, the ICAS Property Manager, and his team modelled the ICAS sweaters on a daily basis in the Institute.

The only other legal problem arose some years later, as a result of our application for registration of the CA brand, when the French bank, Crédit Agricole, threatened to block the application and take legal proceedings to prevent ICAS from using the CA logo. During the 1997 World Congress of Accountants in Paris an urgent meeting was held with directors of the Bank, who were persuaded to withdraw their opposition.

The objective of the re-branding initiative was to make the public much more aware of the work and achievements of ICAS and its members and of their role both in public life and in the financial and business world. Previously, much of the public interest activity of ICAS and the work of its members had gone largely unsung.

At the end of 1989, as the re-branding exercise was launched, the membership of ICAS stood at precisely 12,345 – a happy arithmetical coincidence. This relatively small membership base engendered good collegiate spirit and there was, and remains, a strong belief in the concept of small being beautiful. However, in terms of revenue and future viability, this characteristic presented challenges.

This, and a profound belief in the quality of the educational processes, led ICAS to develop a campaign designed to attract students and, at the same time, promote the concept of the membership as *primus inter pares*. The public relations and marketing consultants presented "*The Edge*" as the strap line for this campaign. This campaign proved successful and enduring. It conveyed the idea of the CA and ICAS being at the forefront of the accountancy profession, leading by example and, in the words of the strap line, 'having the edge' on the competition. This and subsequent campaigns were supported by a newly designed CA logo that was used for ICAS letterheads, as the flagstaff for *CA Magazine* and on ICAS merchandise.

In education, the re-launch of the ICAS annual prize giving and graduation ceremony in 1990 was one of the most successful initiatives in the re-branding process. Designed to emphasise the value of the CA qualification and the duties that newly admitted members take on by entering membership, this event has grown annually and is now regarded as one of the highlights of the ICAS calendar.

The ICAS members' services department developed a number of CA branded products for use by members. Currently, these include both services, such as *CA Practitioner Service; CA Consulting;* and *Business Care*, and products under these brands, advertising the various services provided by CAs. In recent years, the CA logo has been emblazoned on two taxis - one in Edinburgh and one in Glasgow.

The law has never offered protection to the designation of 'accountant' and CA practitioners continually asked their Institute to take action to strengthen their position as highly qualified practitioners and to alert the public to the potential dangers of using unqualified self-styled accountants. In response, the leadership of ICAS seized appropriate opportunities to speak to the advantages of consulting

CA practitioners. The Institute assisted groups of CA practitioners to insert corporate advertisements in local newspapers and acetate window stickers displaying the CA logo were also made available to members for display in their office windows and these were widely used.

This concept of ICAS and its members being one step ahead was again suggested by the follow-up campaign that described members as "leading figures in business". This was designed to underline the fact that the CA education and training provided by ICAS in co-operation with its training firms was the best qualification for a career in finance and business, whether as a practitioner advising clients, or as a senior employee in finance, commerce and industry. While retaining the idea of financial skills, this description of our members also supported the contention that CAs were more than highly competent accountants. The epithet badged them as highly skilled professionals with a deep understanding of accounting, finance and business. It also conveyed the message that they belonged to an Institute that was a class leader.

The development and protection of the CA brand was largely a matter of creative thinking by our consultants with a great deal of skill and hard work at staff level. Generally, a great deal of satisfaction was derived from this process. ICAS began to produce highly professional in-house publications and the new design of *CA Magazine* complemented its repositioned editorial policy. The visibility of ICAS was significantly improved and the re-branding initiative led to sponsorship arrangements that enabled ICAS to organise high profile conferences and other events.

We have been careful to monitor the progress of all aspects of the re-branding process, which is a continuing one. Membership surveys, outside research and tracking of media hits have confirmed the success of the process in projecting the qualities and skills of members of ICAS and of the public interest role of ICAS and its work on behalf of the profession.

Peter Johnston was Chief Executive of ICAS from 1989 to 1999 and Chief Executive of IFAC from 1999 until 2001.

Sundries 14: Rugby Triumphs

March 1977 brought more rugby triumphs. 'Our congratulations to W B B Gammell, a CA student with Arthur Young McClelland Moores & Co, Edinburgh', *The Accountant's Magazine* declared, 'who celebrated his first cap for Scotland against Ireland at Murrayfield on February 19 by scoring two tries. Obviously', the report continued, 'the "CA connection" helps Scotland produce winning rugby teams, for also included in that victorious side was W S Watson, CA, an accountant with Microwave & Electronic Systems Ltd, (who was recalled to the side after the debacle at Twickenham). The final score was Scotland 21 – Ireland 18'. These days Gammell is Chief Executive of Cairn Energy.

Whither the Profession? 11: Clarity

Meanwhile by November 1983 David Tweedie had become chief technical partner at Thomson McLintock. This is the conclusion of what he had to say to the ICAS membership on the issue of 'true and fair'.

While the detailed requirements necessary to show a true and fair view will continually evolve as social attitudes and technical skills change, the basic question to be posed by both director and auditor will remain. "If", they should ask, "if I were on 'the outside' and did not have the detailed knowledge of the company's trading position that I have as I look at these accounts, would I be able to obtain a clear and unambiguous picture of that reality from these accounts?". If the picture is poorly painted, or worse, fails to represent reality, then the directors have failed to meet the paramount principle of financial reporting – to show a true and fair view – and must return to their canvas until their picture is a faithful representation of the enterprise's state of affairs and profit or loss.

Scots Outwith 17: Istanbul

In January 1988 Paul Boyle, these days Chief Executive of the Financial Reporting Council, was extolling the virtues of working in Istanbul on behalf of Coopers & Lybrand. 'Accounting practice has been heavily influenced by Turkish tax law', he reported.

It has been my view for some years that, from the standpoint of fair financial reporting, it is misleading to confuse tax accounting and financial reporting. My view has been reinforced by my experiences in Turkey, where the application of strict tax laws can have some unusual accounting consequences. For example, under Turkish tax law it is not acceptable to write off stocks unless they have been physically destroyed in the presence of an inspector from the Ministry of Finance. There are similar difficulties in making provisions for doubtful receivables, although it is not actually necessary for an inspector to attend the debtor's funeral before relief is granted.

Whither the Profession? 12: A Challenge

In June 1988 Ewan Brown CA of Noble Grossart sprang into action upon the publication by ICAS of the ground-breaking research project *Making Corporate Reports Valuable*.

This important discussion document must on no account be allowed to gather dust', he said. 'It is the spark which has the potential to lead accounts and accountants out of the Dark Ages and make relevant and comprehensible the hotchpotch of jargon and mumbo jumbo, the anodyne comments of anonymous chairman and the fudgings and concealments that at present masquerade as "Reports and Accounts". What a challenge!' His enthusiasm remained undimmed. His concluding words were that: 'If the discussion document does nothing else it exposes bluntly and uncompromisingly the total inadequacy of the present system of corporate reporting and reveals, in a tantalising form, what could be achieved by starting afresh. Making Corporate Reports Valuable identifies the various interested parties (managers, auditors, professional accountancy bodies, etc.) but it does not ask or attempt the question which will be asked by each group: "What is in it for us?". If we are to hear the shout "Corporate Reporting is dead; long live Corporate Reporting!" it is vital that satisfactory answers can be given to that question.

Scots Outwith 18: Italian Reforms

In May 1976 it was Ian Marrian, these days ICAS Chief Executive, in tandem with his fellow Deloitte colleague Hugh Christie, suggesting that Italy and its reforming accounting profession was in the need of the integrity of the Scots CA. 'Today's newly qualified CAs should consider the exciting concept of what is happening in Italy now, for here is a situation which arises but once in a lifetime, the enactment of a sweeping new law and the attendant rebirth of the accountancy profession', they said. Parmalat was but a twinkle in someone's eye at the time.

Newfangled 9: Computers Arrive

Under the heading of '*A New Computer for Edinburgh*' members were told in January 1961 that:

> By installing an IBM 305 RAMAC computer Scottish Midland Guarantee Trust Ltd, claims to be the first finance company in the United Kingdom to install a computer. This is the first installation of a machine of this type in Scotland and only the second in the United Kingdom.

Whither the Profession? 13: The Way Ahead

In September 1990 a profile of David Tweedie, newly ensconced as the first-ever Chairman of the independent Accounting Standards Board, showed that he was already gearing up on some themes which would become familiar in the years ahead. 'I have always been interested in financial reporting', he said, 'and as technical partner at Peats I was constantly running up against creative accounting. Having been a critic of this approach to financial reporting I felt I could not turn down an opportunity to try and do something about it'. He was also gearing up for the expected opposition from companies to his Board's views. 'If they can convince us that something is wrong then we will listen', he said. 'If we can be persuaded that our thinking has no relevance to the real world and that a standard has no relationship to the facts of commercial life then we will listen carefully. But if companies have nothing more to their objections than that they do not like what we are up to, then we are unlikely to respond positively'. Even then the line was drawn in the sand. And his ambitions were plain. 'We want to change the entire financial reporting climate', he said. 'We want to take away the pressure for accounts manipulation. We want to get reporting back to a more consistent basis – and that will not be easy'.

Newfangled 10: Mini-Computers

'Accounting Machine or Computer?' was the heading for an announcement in June 1975. 'A successful course on this topic presented in Edinburgh on May 21 included the demonstration of equipment which bridged the data processing gap between accounting machines and mini-computers. This was the first PQE course to include such a demonstration. Two excellent lectures gave the arguments for and against using either an accounting machine or a computer in two different types of organisation'.

Newfangled 11: Telex

Another technological breakthrough was reported in October 1976. Under the headline: *Institute installs 'Telex'* a story recounted that :

> *"Telex" has recently been installed at the premises of the Institute's Secretariat, at 27 Queen Street, Edinburgh. Telexes have also been installed at the headquarters of the English and Irish Institutes of Chartered Accountants. This new facility should lead to a considerable improvement in the communications between the three chartered bodies, enabling the process of consultation and the exchange of information to be speeded up and costs to be reduced.*

The note was illustrated by a photograph of a beaming 'Mr E H V McDougall', then the Institute's Secretary, as he 'looks on as Mrs Anne Buchanan, a member of the Institute's staff, transmits messages of greeting on the new telex from the ICAS President, Mr A B Richards, CA,' (sporting a wry smile), 'to the Presidents of the English and Irish Institutes'.

Scots Outwith 19: Harvard

Norman Murray, these days ICAS junior vice-president, reported back from his business studies at Harvard in June 1988.

> *Harvard Business School Professors talked of accountants simply as "accountants" or "bookkeepers" and, at times provocatively, as "bean-counters". To them the real world of finance was embodied in an MBA, and my own impression of the standing of CPAs in the US was that they were significantly less well regarded than Chartered Accountants are in the UK.*

The seeds of Enron had been spotted early.

Sundries 15: Decency

At the 1984 Summer School Robert Courtney Smith, these days Sir Robert Smith (now retired), told of his early auditing days in the 1950s. 'He recalled a time', it was reported in *Accountancy Age*, 'when the vouching for an audit was nowhere near complete by the time the client wanted to have the accounts signed. The audit partner justified the early signing and the effective abandonment of the audit by telling his junior of the client: "Och, they're decent people"'.

The Swansong of The Summer School

In September 1996 what was to be the last Summer School was held. This is what Robert Bruce wrote in *The Times* that week:

There can be joy in accountancy. Anyone who was at last week's annual ICAS summer conference in St Andrews would understand that. It has become a unique occasion in the accounting calendar. It is a time for Scots accountants to get together, to listen to some of the best business and financial thoughts of the day, to discuss the issues and to have a thoroughly good time. This year saw three stunning case studies. Ian Russell, Scottish Power's finance director, Brian Stewart, Scottish & Newcastle chief executive, and Derek Hunt, the chairman of MFI, made a powerful trio. All gave their thoughts on growth and strategy and how their organisations had approached those challenges. The point about such quality of contributors and how the conference brings out the best in them is the concentration on relaxing. Each of the talks is mulled over by discussion groups in private and ideas brought to plenary session to draw the speakers' comments. It is not a formal business environment so people like Derek Hunt speak more directly and plainly than normally. The value is immense. The discussion groups embrace a wide range of experience. In one there was a gap of almost 60 years between the qualification dates of two participants. Sir Ian Morrow, the legendary company doctor, qualified as a Scots CA in 1936. The youngest of the group qualified with a lively Edinburgh firm only last year. Sir Ian passed on anecdotes of experience to illustrate topics such as the dearth of entrepreneurs with staying power in Scotland. The newly-qualified CA told him how the exam system could be reformed. The groups provide low-key but informed discussion. Having Derek Hunt sit in and talk about the importance of cashflow taught people more

*about how management really works than any business school course
ever could. And there is, of course, the social side. The Scots institute
is a small accounting body. Its members stick together and build close
networks. There is still the end of conference ceilidh – post dinner
entertainment created by the members. People bring fiddles and play
jigs. Others create sketches and songs. This year's highlight was
probably the dramatic re-creation, involving the president and chief
executive of the Canadian ICA of The Shooting of Dan McGrew.
Though the appearance of the Scots chief executive, Peter Johnston,
as the vengeful miner, "with a face most hair and the dreary stare of
a dog whose day is done" upstaged them both. The evening, by now
teetering on morning, ends with piping and dancing. In short, the
conference is the sort of event that leaves people happier and wiser.
And that may be its problem. For conferences like this, which take a
couple of days or more out of the diary, have fallen foul of the frenetic
insistence on avoiding thought. The large accounting firms, whose
natural habitat such events used to be, now encourage a culture where
a combination of astonishing and burgeoning internal bureaucracy
combined with an insistence on exclusive loyalty measured almost
solely through long hours has eradicated the thoughtful. The result
is that fewer and fewer accountants feel that they can justify not
being at their desk for more than a few hours. This is crushing the
profession. Events such as this are the ones that give you time to gain
new ideas and reassess old ones. The insistence by the accountancy
firms in particular that such processes are superfluous is a criminal
and pernicious destruction of the central value of the profession. It is
significant that the institute president, Robert Smith, chief executive
of Morgan Grenfell Development Capital, spoke with great passion
to members. He had been in London overnight heading the internal
investigation into Morgan Grenfell's European Fund. He talked
generally about the essence of being a professional. "Be dead honest.
Be dead straight and blow whistles. A system is growing up which*

*says that if there is a manual then you have covered yourself and
your actions. Right and wrong don't seem to exist any more. And
we all know in our hearts when something is right or wrong". Those
principles are what an event like the Scots summer conference builds.
Long may it flourish.*

Needless to say it was the last year in which the Summer School
was held.

Sundries 16: Speyside

In April 2001 Grenville Johnston, one of the more entertaining of
ICAS Presidents, set the scene for his final presidential letter to members
by topping it with a photograph of himself at around the age of two
or three. He then introduced members to the new ICAS tartan.

*I have already ordered my trews and waistcoat and I hope that you
will make a point of obtaining articles made from it. If you have not
been eligible to wear the tartan up until now, and you are a member
of ICAS, then here is your chance.*

His final message was that:

*To be honest with you all, I have had a fun year. I will admit to
being a might tired and a touch overweight, but I have travelled to
places I have never been to and constantly met delightful people.*

He signed off with the sort of Highland PS which had characterised
his communications with members.

*Spey, (the puppy), has entered our lives with a vengeance. Jocky
the cat is not pleased. Mrs Johnston is definitely being tested! Spey,
(the river), gave me a superb day in early March. Two kelts, (spent
salmon), got the rod bent and the line tight. There is going to be
life after the presidency!*

Newfangled 12: Websites!

'This month', it was announced in May 1999, 'there are no prizes for spotting what's new on the ICAS website'. Amongst other things 'A Student Noticeboard with several non-accounting jokes has also been included, for a bit of light relief amidst the serious stuff'. The overall website was said to be more 'user-friendly'. 'But it's an on-going process and, to be successful, it's got to be customer-driven. So please, tell us what you think and what you want – we'll do our best to provide'.

Whither the Profession? 14: Enron Breaks

When Cahal Dowds took up his position as the youngest President in the history of ICAS in April 2002 he must have been cursing the Americans. His mission was turned upside down. The only thing the outside world wanted to know about accountants was how had the Enron scandal happened and what were they going to do about it. Doubtless taking a deep breath before writing his first monthly letter to members Dowds said that:

> *The world has changed forever and it affects us all. The bankruptcy of Enron, the largest corporate failure in the history of the USA, if not the world, has raised the serious question: was this collapse resultant of a failure of an unconventional business model or fraud on a massive scale? This is a complex issue and, of course, it will take time for conclusions to be reached, but it is no exaggeration to say that throughout the world the accounting profession faces the greatest crisis in its history. It is the role of our Institute to play a*

meaningful part in the ensuing debate. Our Institute must listen to our members and, in recommending change, weigh carefully any unintended consequences which might flow from "quick fixes". Our Institute must be courageous, open to learn and to support change where improvements can be made in the public interest. Equally we must have no fear of being accused of being defensive if we disagree with views that we believe simply to be wrong. True reform requires respect for differing views resulting in outcomes that are measured and considered.

He also went on to say that:

The core of this whole issue, which is critical to our profession, and that which supports our brand, is quality and integrity. The Enron saga is a stark reminder to us all that a business can survive lost customers, it can survive the loss of people, but it cannot survive the loss of reputation.

Making Corporate Reports Valuable

BY

Paul Boyle

Introduction

The British have a sentimental admiration for the tradition of the "gentleman amateur" in the world of sport: mountaineers in tweed jackets, skiers with leather bindings and "Brylcreem" heroes who played top division football in the winter and first class cricket in the summer. The passing of those days is mourned by some but most of us accept the inevitability of professionalisation.

In the history of the accounting profession there is also a long-standing tradition of the "gentleman amateur". For the first 125 years or so of the accountancy profession's existence, all significant developments in accounting thought and techniques were the product of the gifted practitioner – there were very few Professors of Accountancy and the concept of a "professional standard-setter" simply did not exist. The thought-leaders were also the leading practitioners of their day; the names of Bogie, Flint, Morrison and Shaw come to mind. *The Accountant's Magazine* (as it used to be called) regularly published articles on technical issues contributed by practising accountants.

The 21st century is an era of professionalisation in accounting and auditing thought. There are several major standard-setting organisations around the world all of which have substantial numbers of full-time paid staff; and the standards which they produce are increasingly lengthy, complex in their reasoning and technical in their language. The Professors of Accountancy in the UK could now fill the Chamber of the Scottish Parliament – but a translation service would be required for the average practitioner to understand what they were discussing. Few practitioners today would have the confidence – even if they had the inclination – to contribute a serious technical article to a professional journal.

Making Corporate Reports Valuable, a Discussion Document published by the Research Committee of ICAS in 1988, is perhaps one of the last, but arguably one of the most influential, examples of amateurism in the development of accounting thought. Viewed from a distance of only 16 years it is astonishing in its boldness of ambition, breadth of scope and simplicity of language. This is one view of how it came to be written and the impact that it has had.

The origins of the project

ICAS has had a Research Committee for many years. The Committee, consisting of around a dozen members of varied ages and experience, typically acted as a commissioning body, inviting authors (increasingly academics) to undertake research projects. It has had a tradition of encouraging research into topics which are likely to be of practical interest to Institute members rather than some of the more obscure topics which find their way into the academic journals.

In 1985 the Committee, under its Convener, Sir John (as he then wasn't) Shaw, was meeting in 27 Queen Street to consider what should be on its future work programme. The discussion took place against the background of a prolonged period of high inflation and a number of high profile corporate scandals in which the reliability of the published accounts had been called into question. One of the Committee members noted that it was ten years since the publication by the English Institute of *The Corporate Report*, which had been an earlier attempt at a "blank sheet of paper" review of accounting; what about assessing its impact on practice? Sir (as he then wasn't) David

Tweedie, who was a member of the Committee, recalls that he had been watching the antics of a squirrel in Queen Street Gardens when the Convener asked for his opinion and he blurted out something along the lines of: "the accounting model in use today is completely broken and needs to be re-built from scratch".

This idea found considerable support amongst the Committee who modestly decided that they would rise to the re-building challenge. In a departure from their normal *modus operandi* the Committee decided that it itself should tackle the project rather than commission someone to do it.

How the Report was written

The Committee re-convened a few weeks later for an Away Day at Peebles Hydro at which the scope of the project was mapped out. The Committee's enthusiasm was re-inforced and various working parties were established to look at different aspects of the project. Mindful of their own title, the Committee commissioned a few academics to undertake a review of the literature on a number of topics, including the vexed topic of alternatives to the historic cost basis of measurement.

Over the following two years the majority of the Committee's time was spent on the project and the working parties met at odd hours and in odd locations in addition to the Committee's normal meetings.

The literature surveys were reviewed; any conclusions which were inconsistent with the Committee's ideas were disregarded. A preliminary version of the Committee's conclusions was presented to Institute members at the Summer School in St Andrews in 1987; after a few drams the reception received did not seem so bad. A "test to destruction" event took place later that year at which the conclusions were presented to a highly critical group of hard-nosed senior members in business and senior academics; undeterred the Committee pressed on.

Peter McMonnies, a former technical partner from Thomson McLintock & Co, was coaxed out of retirement to edit the texts produced by the working parties into a coherent document. Peter's contribution to the project was crucial. After much debate a title was agreed: *Making Corporate Reports Valuable* was a pun, as one of the Committee's more controversial recommendations was that historical cost accounting should be replaced by net realisable value.

In 1988 the Council of the Institute consented to the publication of the Discussion Document, but they were highly nervous of the reception which it might receive and insisted that it be published in the name of the Research Committee rather than as an official ICAS publication.

The scope of the Discussion Document

The Committee stated that its objective was "to improve, in the long-term, the quality of measuring and reporting corporate activity".

The Discussion Document's recommendations covered external reporting (of both financial and non-financial information), internal reporting (particularly information presented to boards of directors), auditing (which it re-named "independent assessment") and corporate governance (it pre-dated the Cadbury Report by four years). This was a lot to cover in 90 paperback pages!

The Document's foundations included the key propositions that:

- financial reports ought to portray economic reality; and

- the information needed by investors is the same in kind, but not in volume, as that needed by management.

The Document is clear that corporate reports at that time were unsatisfactory because they concentrated on:

- legal form rather than on economic substance;
- the past to the exclusion of the future;
- cost rather than on value; and
- profit rather than wealth.

The Committee then proceeded to make its recommendations on the basis that it could ignore existing laws, accounting standards and other constraints, which certainly made radicalism a lot easier.

MCRV's impact on corporate reporting practice

The recommendations in *MCRV*, many of which seemed very radical at the time of their publication, have had a significant impact on corporate reporting practice. Amongst the recommendations which have been implemented are:

- "managements (*sic*) should not give information to analysts which they do not give to other external users at the same time" (incorporated into the rules of the UK Listing Authority).
- "information coming before boards of directors ought to be … comprehensive" (Combined Code on Corporate Governance).
- "the timeliness of corporate reports could be improved by electronic distribution methods" (extensive use of the internet by companies).
- "there should be … reporting of 'events' as they occur" (UKLA rules).
- "Every corporate report should contain a Statement of Objectives" (guidance on Operating and Financial Review issued by the Accounting Standards Board).

- "segmental information should be given" (Statement of Standard Accounting Practice 25).
- "Related parties should be identified and significant transactions with them disclosed" (Financial Reporting Standard 8).
- "there should be a statement of … innovation" (OFR).
- "merger accounting does [not] provide a true and fair view" (FRS 2).
- "Economic substance should prevail over legal form (particularly in relation to off-balance sheet financing)" (FRS 5).
- "Information on the economic environment [should be published and] should include facts about the market and comparative operational statistics" (OFR).
- "Information should be given … on … the duties of audit committees" (Combined Code).
- "changes in market capitalisation … from period to period should be the subject of comment" (OFR).
- "audit committees, preferably drawn from non-executive directors, should be required for all [listed] companies" (Combined Code).

Readers may speculate on the connection between the extent of *MCRV's* impact on corporate reporting practice and the fact that David Tweedie was the first Chairman of the Accounting Standards Board.

Recommendations in *MCRV* which have not been implemented

Although, as can been seen above, a substantial number of *MCRV's* recommendations have had an impact on practice not all of its recommendations have been implemented. Amongst these are:

- "Information should be given on areas of accounting subject to uncertainty and the boundaries of uncertainty".

- "[net realisable] value is a better basis than cost".

- there should be "a long form … report from the independent assessor" (the Committee's proposed successor to present-day auditors).

It is a matter of opinion as to whether some of the more recent cases of accounting controversy might not have been alleviated were these recommendations now part of corporate reporting practice.

Conclusions

There is substantial evidence that *MCRV* has influenced the development of corporate reporting practice.   *MCRV* is extensively quoted in the academic literature. A search for "*Making Corporate Reports Valuable*" on Google yields 142 results. In addition, in the years after *MCRV* was published the Research Committee commissioned a number of further studies, including a prototype as to how *MCRV* might be applied in practice (published under the title of "*Melody plc*").

Notwithstanding the nervousness of the Council at the time, it has enhanced the reputation of ICAS as an organisation which can contribute to thought leadership in the accountancy profession. The success of *MCRV* encouraged the Research Committee a few years later to undertake a similar project focusing on auditing (*Auditing into the Twenty-first Century*). It is gratifying that in its most recent review the Council has determined that thought leadership will be one of the building blocks of ICAS's future strategy. The challenge for ICAS will be to produce future work which is as influential as *MCRV*.

Whatever the future holds for ICAS's contribution to thought leadership, the amateurs of the Research Committee of '85–'88 can look back on a lot of fun and some long-lasting friendships which were made in the course of writing *MCRV*.

Paul Boyle is the first Chief Executive of the newly-expanded Financial Reporting Council. The FRC aims to promote confidence in corporate reporting and governance. Previously Paul was the Chief Operating Officer of the Financial Services Authority and was with Cadbury Schweppes for eight years. He trained with Coopers & Lybrand in Glasgow and spent eight years with the firm, including two years in Turkey. His first job in industry was with WH Smith Group plc.

Whither the Profession? 15: Aftermath

In April 2003 Cahal Dowds, President of ICAS throughout the aftermath of Enron, wrote his final message to members.

Forgive me,

he started,

> *if, in my last President's Comment, I take time out to reflect on the past year. Of course it all started with the Enron and WorldCom scandals in the US. Initially these scandals were dismissed as aberrations which did not reflect the state of the corporate world. But as we all know, we don't tend to find one cockroach in a kitchen. Global Crossing quickly followed and when Dennis Kozlowski, former chief executive of Tyco, was indicted on charges of corruption, the sheer number of headline grabbing scandals made those initial arguments difficult to justify. The accounting profession was on the front page. Even Private Eye, on its July 2002 front cover, had the headline "New Osama Threat to America", "Forget Terrorism, I'm Going to Become an Accountant".*

Dowds concluded that:

> *Last year's shocking events evidenced a lack of ethical standards and, when combined with a culture of short-termism, this is a recipe for disaster. We must always remember to put ethics first. Over the past year I have emphasised the constant need for integrity. This need will always remain as, regretfully, will the prevalence of short-termism and all the ensuing pressures associated with it.*

Scots Outwith 20: Iraq

The tradition of the far-flung CA was being upheld in 2004, as an anonymous account of life in war-torn Baghdad published in *CA Magazine* showed. The writer was there to set up a finance operation for a multi-national. 'There is a direct route to Baghdad but the centre section has no tarmac', he reported. 'I travelled it once and the dust thrown up by the cars was so dense that when another vehicle passed you were in a white-out for three or four hundred metres. The route passes no towns. Towns are dangerous places, though the only place I was shot at was on that desert route when we came across a burning container truck. If a truck in a convoy under escort breaks down on the desert road it is torched rather than leaving it to the mercies of the local inhabitants.

Between Ad Diwiniyah and Baghdad, the desert gave way to flat farmland which reminded me of Lincolnshire. The Euphrates runs through the area and excellent irrigation systems allow small agricultural units to flourish far into the desert'. Once in Baghdad:

> *You don't think about the possibility of being blown up – the threat is in the back of your mind but you don't think it will happen to you.*

After three weeks he was moved out of the Palestine Hotel.

> *Just as well, - the Palestine was attacked with mortars soon afterwards. Americans are nervous about harming innocent civilians, but Iraqi guards who do not know the driver of a vehicle or a person approaching on foot open fire. Many's the night we sat on the roof of the hotel having a sundowner and found ourselves in the middle of a gun-fight with bullets bouncing off the building as our guards opened up on someone approaching our no-go area. Around October the suicide*

bombing and the mortaring started in earnest. You would hear the crump of a bomb somewhere in the city. One explosion scared the hell out of me. I was on the roof of the hotel, about to phone my wife, when the car bomb at the Red Cross centre exploded. It was at least five kilometres away but the violence of that explosion left me stunned and shaken.

He reported on life outside Baghdad.

I had to do a lot of travelling. In the towns people appeared to be living normal lives. The markets were full: not only with abundant food, but the trappings of Western life, piled high – satellite dishes, refrigerators, freezers, televisions, cookers, ghetto-blasters. And people were buying them – stuffing them into the back of old cars or piling them high on pickups. The dollar was the currency and as more and more people started working for the coalition more and more dollars were in circulation. I was paying over $750,000 (£409,000) a month to Iraqi businessmen from my little office.

He was optimistic.

The Iraqis I worked with just wanted normality – a job, a home, education, travel, money for food and the little luxuries denied them for so long. They are hard-working people with good business sense and I am confident that once security returns to the streets, the Iraqi economy will outgrow every other in the Middle East. There will be excellent business opportunities – everything is 15 years out of date.

He ended his recollections with a simple

thank you and apologies to my wife and children. I had no right to put you through all that anxiety.

The Distaff Side 7: Longevity

In September 1996 the President, Robert Smith, was sending out the traditional congratulatory messages to members who had reached significant anniversaries in their length of membership. One member was being congratulated on completing 70 years in practice.

'The lady concerned is 99 years old' he reported, 'and furthermore the message had to be delivered to her office because she was at work'.

TIMELINE

	ICAS Events	Accountancy Events	World Events
1854	Incorporation by Royal Charter of– The Society of Accountants in Edinburgh. The description "Chartered Accountant" devised and adopted.		Crimean War begins. Income Tax raised to 1s. 2d. in £.
1855	Designatory letters "CA" devised and adopted. Incorporation by Royal Charter of – The Institute of Accountants and Actuaries in Glasgow.		
1856		The Bankruptcy (Scotland) Act.	
1858			The crown assumes the government of India.
1862		The Companies Act introduces, in table A, a model, optional, audit clause.	
1867	Incorporation by Royal Charter of– The Society of Accountants in Aberdeen.		
1873	Glasgow Institute purchases its first premises (in West Nile Street).		

	ICAS Events	Accountancy Events	World Events
1877			Queen Victoria proclaimed Empress of India.
1880		Incorporation by Royal Charter of the Institute of Chartered Accountants in England and Wales.	
1885		Incorporation of Institute of Chartered Accountants in Ireland.	
1891	Edinburgh Society purchases 27 Queen Street ("the CA Rooms").		
1892	Formation of the Scottish Chartered Accountants' General Examining Board.		
1896	First edition of *The Official Directory of the Chartered Accountants of Scotland*.		
1897	First issue of *The Accountants' Magazine*.		Queen Victoria's diamond Jubilee.
1899	Formation of the Association of Scottish Chartered Accountants in London.		
1900		The Companies Act introduces compulsory audit.	

	ICAS Events	Accountancy Events	World Events
1902	Formation of a standing Joint Committee of the Councils of the various UK Societies of Chartered Accountants.		
1904		First International Congress of Accountants held in St Louis.	
1908		The Companies Act introduces private companies.	
1913		The Bankruptcy (Scotland) Act.	
1914			The First World War begins.
1915	Formation of the Joint Committee of Councils of the Chartered Accountants of Scotland.		
1917			Revolution in Russia.
1919	First golf competition for the Moore Cup. Inaugural lecture by the first Professor of Accounting and Business Method in the University of Edinburgh.		The Sex Disqualification (Removal) Act.

	ICAS Events	Accountancy Events	World Events
1923	Admission of first female Scottish Chartered Accountant and first female Chartered Accountant qualified by examination (Miss I.C. Guthrie – later Mrs Lochhead).		
1926	Inaugural lecture by the first Johnstone Smith Professor of Accountancy, Glasgow University.		The General Strike.
1929		The Companies Act introduces holding companies.	The Great Crash on Wall Street.
1933			Adolf Hitler becomes Reichskanzler.
1939			The Second World War begins.
1945	Sub- Committee formed to discuss merging the three Societies of Scottish Chartered Accountants.		Atom bombs dropped on Hiroshima and Nagasaki.
1947			Partition of India and Pakistan.

	ICAS Events	Accountancy Events	World Events
1948		The Companies Act introduces-compulsory reporting by auditors on profit and loss accounts, recognition of professional accountancy qualifications for appointments of auditors, group accounts.	
1951	Edinburgh Society's name changed to "The Institute of Chartered Accountants of Scotland" and amalgamation of the three Scottish Societies.	The Accountants Joint Parliamentary Committee in existence. Union Européenne des experts comptable, economiques et financiers (UEC) formed.	ECSC formed.
1952		6th International Congress of Accountants, London.	
1953	First Summer School of ICAS. Lister Committee appointed.	Some proposals of Audio-visual Aids Committee approved.	
1954–5	Centenary Celebrations Edinburgh and Glasgow.		
1956			Suez crisis.

	ICAS Events	Accountancy Events	World Events
1957		The Society of Incorporated Accountants dissolved – members join one or other of the three Institutes of Chartered Accountants. The Chartered Accountants Joint Standing Committee formed. 7th International Congress of Accountants, Amsterdam.	Treaty of Rome signed.
1959	The "Lister Committee Rules" adopted (academic year, *etc*). First ICAS Course on Computers.		
1960	First " CA Academic Year" starts.	Observers from ICAS, ICAEW and NIVRA attend UEC Congress, Zurich.	
1962	ICAS Future Policy Committee reports.	8th International Congress of Accountants, New York City.	Beatles first single.
1963	ICAS Research programme begins.	The "new members" join UEC under its revised constitution. European Congress of Accountants, Edinburgh.	Assassination in Dallas of US President John F Kennedy.

	ICAS Events	Accountancy Events	World Events
1964	Dewar Committee appointed.	JDipMA Scheme launched. "Integration" talks start. UEC Congress, Vienna.	
1965		The Finance Act.	
1966		First UEC Study Conference, Baden-Baden.	World Cup success for England.
1967	Dewar Committee's report adopted.	9th International Congress of Accountants, Paris. International Committee formed.	Summer of Love. Scotland become first team to beat English World Cup winners.
1968			Treaty of Rome becomes operative.
1969	North Berwick Conference on Education. Charles Committee report.	ICAEW, ICAS and ICAI form Accounting Standards Steering Commttee (ASSC). UEC Congress, Copenhagen.	
1970		Failure of "Integration" proposals.	England's footballers "fail" in Mexico.
1971		Second UEC Study Conference, London.	

	ICAS Events	Accountancy Events	World Events
1972	The Charles Committee's proposals approved.	10th International Congress of Accountants, Sydney. International Committee becomes ICCAP.	Pocket calculator introduced.
1973	The new ICAS education scheme starts.	UK, Irish and Danish representatives join Bureau elargi of Groupe d'Etudes. UEC Congress, Madrid. International Accounting Standards Committee (IASC) formed.	UK, Ireland and Denmark join EEC. Yom Kippur War.
1974	Committees and staff re-deployed.	CCAB formed. IAS 1 issued.	US President Nixon resigns.
1975	Rowan House opened. St Vincent Street premises sold and part leased back.	Ethical Guides issued. "The Corporate Report" published. Third UEC Study Conference, Yugoslavia.	The Sandilands Report published.
1976	Victor McDougall, Secretary of ICAS, Editor-in-Chief of *The Accountant's Magazine* and author of *Fifth Quarter Century*, retires. Auditing Practices Committee formed.	ASSC becomes ASC. Inflation Accounting Steering Group (IASG) formed.	

	ICAS Events	Accountancy Events	World Events
1977	*Pioneers of a Profession* by JG Stewart published. SCATE launches appeal for funds for new educational centre in Edinburgh, Stewart House.	International Federation of Accountants (IFAC) is founded.	First Star Wars film.
1978	Professor David Tweedie appointed ICAS Technical Director.		First test-tube baby born.
1979	*The Audit Report – what it says and what it means* by Professor Jack Shaw published. Construction of Stewart House completed.	Ernst and Whinney is formed.	Margaret Thatcher becomes Prime Minister.
1980	*Fifth Quarter Century* by Victor McDougall published.	ACCA's Vera di Palma becomes the first female president of an international accounting body.	The US boycotts the Moscow Olympics.
1981	Ian Marrian appointed Director General of Education. *The Impact of Change on the Accountancy Profession* by Professor David Flint published.		IBM Personal Computer launched.
1982			Falklands War.

	ICAS Events	Accountancy Events	World Events
1983	ICAS Antiquarian Collection formally handed over to the National Library of Scotland.		Launch of the Compact Disc.
1984	Institute's own computing centre, a major development for student education department, established.	Merger of Deloitte, Haskins & Sells and Price Waterhouse falls through.	Miners strike begins. Scotland win rugby Grand Slam.
1985	London training centre opened.		Live Aid makes millions for Africa.
1986		Peat Marwick International and KMG merger forms KPMG.	Chernobyl disaster.
1987		FEE formed (successor to UEC).	First Rugby Union World Cup (New Zealand win). Black Monday on NYSE.
1988	*Making Corporate Reports Valuable* published. *CA Student* magazine first published.	Dearing Committee publishes *The Making of Accounting Standards*.	Ben Johnson breaks record for 100 metres (illegally).

	ICAS Events	Accountancy Events	World Events
1989	Frank Harding CA appointed to IFAC council. *A Strategy for the Future* published. Proposal for A British Institute. Merger with ICAEW rejected.	Ernst & Young is formed from Ernst & Whinney and Arthur Young. Touche Ross, Deloitte Haskins & Sells and Tohmatsu & Co merge to form Deloitte Touche Tohmatsu. In the UK and some other countries Deloitte merged with Coopers & Lybrand instead.	Fall of the Berlin Wall.
1990	*The Way Forward* published.	The Guinness Four are found guilty of fraud. FRC formed and ASB replaces ASC.	John Major replaces Thatcher as Prime Minister. Scotland win rugby Grand Slam.
1991	CAJEC established.	Robert Maxwell drowns. BCCI collapses. Polly Peck and Coloroll scandals lead to Sir Adrian Cadbury's report on corporate governance. Auditing Practices Board formed.	The Warsaw Pact officially dissolved.
1992			Bill Clinton becomes US President.

	ICAS Events	Accountancy Events	World Events
1993	ICAS in Russian joint venture with Stirling University. ICAS Romanian joint venture with Coopers and Lybrand. *Auditing into the Twenty-first Century* published.		
1994	*The Operating and Financial Review: views of analysts and institutional investors* published. Primrose McCabe becomes first woman President.		Nelson Mandela becomes president of South Africa.
1995		Deloitte & Touche creates Deloitte Consulting. Barings collapses.	
1996	Launch of Success in Practice. Last Summer School held.	KPMG produces first annual report by an accountancy firm.	EU ban on British beef.
1997	Centenary issue of CA Magazine (TAM).		Dolly the Sheep 'born'.

	ICAS Events	Accountancy Events	World Events
1998		Coopers & Lybrand and Price Waterhouse form Pricewaterhouse-Coopers. JDS turn the spotlight on Arthur Andersen in connection with the £50 million overstatement of profits by Wickes.	France win the football World Cup.
1999	Queen Street and Stewart House premises sold. ICAS becomes first accounting body to appoint lay members to Council.		Opening of the Scottish Parliament. Launch of Euro.
2000	ICAS moves to Haymarket HQ. *Twenty Seven Queen Street* by Sam McKinstry published.	European Commission announces in July that it intends to make IAS mandatory from 2005. The IASC completes its three year restructuring programme and creates the International Accounting Standards Board, effective from April 2001.	George W Bush becomes US president.

	ICAS Events	Accountancy Events	World Events
2001	Institute's rules amended with effect from 2001 to require the council to appoint two non-accountants as lay members.	SEC's Enron investigation begins. Big Five issue a joint statement in December insisting that self-regulation remains the best policy.	September 11th attacks on US.
2002	Introduction of online annual return and subscription payment.	Andersen's Houston office admits to shredding documents relating to Enron. WorldCom is accused of $4 billion fraud which drags Andersen into another scandal. Andersen global firm implodes. Andersen UK acquired by Deloitte.	Euro becomes legal tender.
2003	*Fast Forward to 2010* published.	Deloitte Touche Tohmatsu rebrands as simply 'Deloitte'.	Iraq War.
2004	ICAS 150th Anniversary.	The Financial Reporting Council is revamped. Inland Revenue merges with Customs and Excise.	Madrid train bombings.

MEMBERSHIP STATISTICS

Admissions and Total Membership - 1864 - 2004

Year	Total Members
1864	146
1874	195
1884	317
1894	542
1900	720
1910	1,432
1920	1,686
1930	3,138
1940	4,556
1950	5,071
1955	5,873
1960	6,823
1965	7,597
1970	8,608
1975	9,308
1980	10,368
1985	11,353
1990	12,609
1995	14,006
2000	14,888
2004	15,558

2004

Worldwide by Employment

Location	In Practice	In Industry	Retired	Others	Total	%
Scotland	2,842	4,245	1,684	708	9,479	61%
Rest of UK	888	1,739	953	376	3,956	25%
Overseas	429	1,148	358	188	2,123	14%

Worldwide by Location

UK	Europe	Africa	Americas	Asia	Oceania
13,435	434	148	797	311	433
86%	3%	1%	5%	2%	3%

Members Located in 98 countries - 2,123 members

Members in Europe: 434

Members in EU: 330

Top Five Overseas Countries	Total
Australia	372
USA	335
Canada	269
Hong Kong	115
South Africa	87